PRAISE FOR THE BALLROOM DANCE COACH

"**The Ballroom Dance Coach** combines expert advice, dance strategies, and life tips to help dancers reach their ultimate level of performance. Jessika's unique ability to weave together reflection exercises, content, and tips make this a one of a kind resource for anyone who wants to reach their personal best in the ballroom world."

– **SAM SODANO,** Owner of the Ohio Star Ball

"You can have two left feet as I do and still delight in Jessika's expert and inspiring coaching. She lights your fire and fans the flames, propelling you to the next level of your life and passions. I dare you to read this enthralling book and not dance with absolute joy!"

– **DEBBIE PHILLIPS,** Founder of Women on Fire® and author of *Women on Fire: 20 Inspiring Women Share Their Life Secrets (and Save You Years of Struggle!)*

"The best of life is often found in experiences that combine mind and body. Here is a terrific book that coaches the reader with rhythm and grace through the mental discipline to become a first-class dancer -- and it will undoubtedly help the reader in all endeavors!"

– **BILL DIFFENDERFFER,** author of *The Samurai Leader: Winning Business Battles with the Wisdom, Honor and Courage of the Samurai Code*

"It takes courage to challenge the status quo, to rise above your fear and self-doubts, and dare to be more than you have until now. Wherever you are - in your dancing, your career or life – the insights and strategies Jessika shares in this unique book will give you the clarity, confidence and courage to get to the next level...and beyond! Buy it, read it, dance it, live it!"

– **MARGIE WARRELL,** Bestselling Author of *Find Your Courage: 12 Acts for Becoming Fearless in Work & Life* (McGraw-Hill), Courage Coach and Keynote Speaker

"These strategies will help anyone looking to improve their performance. Jessika's engaging style of writing and her ability to get experts to share their vast experience in bit-sized nuggets is amazing."

– **YAKOV SMIRNOFF,** Famous Russian comedian, actor, and former advisor to President Ronald Reagan

THE BALLROOM DANCE COACH: EXPERT STRATEGIES TO TAKE YOUR DANCING TO THE NEXT LEVEL

Copyright © 2011 Jessika Ferm. All rights reserved.

→ Published by: **MacCartier Publishing**, a division of J.Ferm, LLC Columbus, OH

→ Editor: **Kacy Cook**

→ Book design, cover and chapter photography by: **Jaime Santillán**
   www.jsantillan.com
   Copyright © 2011 Jaime Santillán Photography. All rights reserved.

→ Additional photography credits:

Christina Donelson:	©Elizabeth Reed
Brendan Donelson:	©Alliance Video & Photography, Inc.
Maureen Andrews:	©Chuck Eddy
Pamela Bolling:	© Michael Caims
Jeffrey Goltiao:	© Stephen Marino
Bill Sparks:	©Karina Wetherbee Photography

All rights reserved. No part of this book may be reproduced or transmitted in any form or by any means, electronic or mechanical, including photocopying, recording or by any information storage and retrieval system, without written permission from the author, except for brief quotations attributed to Jessika Ferm embodied in literary articles or reviews.

This publication is designed to provide accurate and authoritative information in regard to the subject matter covered. It is sold with the understanding that the published is not engaged in rendering professional services. If legal, accounting, medical, psychological or any other expert assistance is required, the services of a competent professional person should be sought. Author and publisher specifically disclaim any liability for the reader's use of any forms or advice provided in this book. It is not warranted as fit for any specific use or purpose, but is intended to give general information that is as current as possible as of the date of publication. Anecdotal and case study names have been changed to protect identities.

First edition
ISBN-13: 978-0-9833700-0-0
Library of Congress Control Number: 2011902726
Printed in the United States of America

How to order:

Copies may be ordered by contacting J.Ferm, LLC, or visiting
http://www.nextleveldancing.com

Quantity discounts available by calling **614-441-8972** or emailing
books@nextleveldancing.com

TO MY DANCING PEEPS,

WITHOUT WHOSE SUPPORT AND ENCOURAGEMENT

THIS BOOK WOULD STILL BE ANOTHER

GREAT DREAM UNREALIZED.

ACKNOWLEDGMENTS

THIS BOOK IS TRULY A COLLABORATION OF LOVE AND PERSEVERANCE that wouldn't have been possible without the support of my dear friends and the generous encouragement and assistance of my extended dancing community. While I can't individually list all of those who offered their time, feedback, and insight, I want to offer a collective "thank you" to everyone who has been involved. Without your energy and enthusiasm, this book would still be just another idea in my head.

There are, however, a few people who must be singled out: Jim Jones for sharing the initial framework and the Stages of Change; Barbara Wayman for always inspiring me to think bigger and never settle for being just "good"; Jeffrey Goltiao, my instructor and friend, who insisted that this book needed to be written; Bill Sparks and Bonita Brockert for inspiring me to become the dancer I aspire to be; and Sam Sodano, the most generous person I know in the ballroom business.

I FEEL SO BLESSED to know all of you. I also acknowledge my Dance Plus Ballroom friends. You are my inspiration and support. I'm so glad I walked in and signed up for that introductory package all those months ago. My life is forever changed, and I don't know how I lived so long without you. Thank you Ron, Linda, and David for sustaining our dance family for more than 30 years.

I AM GRATEFUL to Laura Benton, my fellow dance friend, for proofreading my manuscript and helping me to move the book from inception to finished product. I owe Bill Diffenderffer a merengue for challenging my concepts and pushing me to write the best book possible. My little sister Fanny reminded me that sisterhood knows no boundaries. One of these days you will be dancing and competing with me here in the United States. I am indebted to Jaime Santillán for the wonderful photos on the cover and for the innovative design and layout of this book. I owe a big thank you to my talented models Rachel Halversen, Candy Riley, Jeffrey Goltiao, and Diego Semprun. Your grace and beauty perfectly depict the true essence of this book.

I would also like to acknowledge Lori Graham, my very first mentor, for encouraging me to look beyond the proverbial "wheat field" to see the mountains and lakes of my future all those years ago. I still use this visual reminder to push myself to reach bigger and more meaningful goals. And Molly Luffy for recognizing my true spirit and gently pushing me toward the hobby that changed my life. And finally, I acknowledge my higher power for leading me down this path and inspiring me to live my true purpose.

THE BALLROOM DANCE COACH:

→ Expert Strategies to Take Your Dancing to the Next Level

by JESSIKA FERM

TABLE OF CONTENTS

INTRODUCTION

CHAPTER 1: THE NATURAL STAGES OF CHANGE / pg 1

- Stage 1: Unconscious Incompetence: We Don't Know What We Don't Know
- Stage 2: Conscious Incompetence: We Know That We Don't Know
- Stage 3: Conscious Competence: We Know That We Know
- Stage 4: Unconscious Competence: It's Second Nature

CHAPTER 2: GETTING THROUGH STAGE 2—THE FIRST TIME / pg 17

- Step 1: Reconnecting with Your Dance Passion
- Step 2: Conducting a Skills and Attitude Audit

CHAPTER 3: GETTING THROUGH STAGE 2—OVER AND OVER AND OVER AGAIN / pg 35

- Step 1: Remind Yourself That You've Been Here Before and You Will Be Again
- Step 2: Control Your Gremlins!
- Step 3: Listen to Your Inner Coach
- Step 4: Identify and Maximize Your Strengths, Then Work on Your Weaknesses
- Step 5: Don't Over Rely on Your Feelings; Seek Out and Trust the Advice of Experts
- Step 6: Embrace Your Own Dancing Journey and Stay on the Path

CHAPTER 4: EMBRACING STAGE 3 / pg 83

- Step 1: Challenge Yourself and Practice Your Craft Daily
- Step 2: Enter a Competition or Hire a Coach to Get Honest and Direct Feedback
- Step 3: Beware of the Dark Side

CHAPTER 5: PUSHING THROUGH STAGE 4 / pg 107

    Step 1:   Pick a Dance, Step, Movement, or Choreography and Fine-tune it
    Step 2:   Find a Dance Mentor (Living or Dead, Near or Far)
    Step 3:   Take a Break to Recharge and Reenergize Your Body and Soul

CHAPTER 6: THE DANCING EXPERTS KEEP IT SHORT AND SWEET / pg 131

    Bonita Brockert
    Pamela Bolling
    Bill Sparks
    Maureen Andrews
    Izabella Jundzill
    Ron Clark
    Linda Carpenter
    Kristen Wheeler
    Pierre Allaire
    Mireille Veilleux
    Brendan Donelson
    Christina Donelson
    Decho Kraev
    Bree Watson
    Sam Sodano
    David Butcher
    Jackie Rogers
    Jeffrey Goltiao
    Barry Bernard
    Becci Bernard

CHAPTER 7: SUMMING IT UP / pg 137

CHAPTER 8: MOVING INTO ACTION / pg 141

    Action Plan for Taking My Dancing to the Next Level

INTRODUCTION

"SOCRATES LEARNED TO DANCE WHEN HE WAS SEVENTY BECAUSE HE FELT THAT AN ESSENTIAL PART OF HIMSELF HAD BEEN NEGLECTED."

—SOURCE UNKNOWN

Ballroom dancing entered my life like a full-blown tornado in the spring of 2009. It didn't come as a gentle breeze, offering me time to reflect on or even process the experience. It stormed in, turning everything upside down, and decided to stay.

For many amateurs, ballroom dancing captures a place in the heart that rational thought can't touch. It is a spiritual affair, at once intoxicating and irresistible. For me, it filled a hole I didn't know I had.

As an executive coach running an international leadership firm based in two cities on two continents, I was working 70 hours a week but was always feeling like I was one step behind. I was burning out and at warp speed. My business coach told me I needed a hobby to balance my insane workweek, but I resisted. I didn't see the value in spending time away from work. Didn't she realize that having fun wouldn't pay the bills?! One day when I was feeling particularly out of balance, I walked into a dance studio near my office and signed up for a lesson. The independent entrepreneur in me wanted to show my coach that she was wrong and I was right.

I can now admit that I was the one who was wrong. After three lessons, I realized that I had been missing out on an essential part of myself. I needed something with the power to unite my body, mind, and soul. Today, ballroom dancing is fulfilling me on every level. As a competing amateur dancer and ballroom entrepreneur, in the center of a supportive community, I spend fewer hours working and more quality time with those I love.

Now, combining my business acumen with my passion for dancing and a desire to share my experiences, I am offering my coaching expertise to individuals interested in taking their dancing to the next level. This book is designed to be a self-directed process, made up of practical exercises, tactical strategies, and indispensable resources. It includes tips and advice from world champions as well as accomplished amateur ballroom dancers, coaches, judges, and competition organizers. They know what it takes to move from where you are to where you want to be, and they are sharing their secrets of success with you.

I hope this book will help you to fulfill your dreams and aspirations, both on and off the dance floor!

THE NATURAL STAGES OF

CHAPTER 1:

CHANGE

"THE IMPORTANT THING IS THIS: TO BE ABLE AT ANY MOMENT TO SACRIFICE WHAT WE ARE FOR WHAT WE COULD BECOME."

— CHARLES DUBOIS

A number of facets must come together to succeed at dancing, including steps, rhythm, strength, stamina, artistry, charisma, athleticism, and partnering. In taking your dancing to a higher level, there will be challenges in each of these areas along the way. You will go through four predictable stages of change that can involve discomfort, possibly pain, and frustration. Why bother?

While our bodies are designed to find a place of homeostasis (the desire to maintain the status quo), our brains rarely enjoy lingering in one place for long. Most of us like to discover new things, visit new places, and encounter new people. If we don't continue to learn and evolve, we begin to feel complacent or even depressed.

To make physical changes, our bodies need to break down old muscles and develop new ones, which causes aches. Similarly, when we adopt new habits, such as learning dance steps or techniques, our minds have to **replace old, familiar programming** with novel thoughts and patterns. This can create mental and emotional distress in the form of insecurity, fear, and resistance.

So to kick your dancing skills up a notch, know that you are going to go through some natural pains, corporeal and spiritual. Throughout this book, I have merged tips and tools for propelling you forward with strategies. I will use the "Stages of Change," a popular business theory, as a framework for illustrating the steps to growth, both on and off the dance floor. While the origin of the Stages of Change (also called the Stages of Learning) is difficult to pinpoint, the concepts have been embraced by experts ranging from prominent psychologist Abraham Maslow to the U.S. Gordon Training International organization.

This chapter lays the foundation for the exercises and advice you will learn in this book. Each stage has unique characteristics, and it is important that you familiarize yourself with them. The majority of the book focuses on Stage 2, which is where we tend to get stuck or start feeling the pains of growth and development. Just remember that we have to go through each stage—some over and over again—to reach our dancing goals.

STAGE 1 / UNCONSCIOUS INCOMPETENCE: WE DON'T KNOW WHAT WE DON'T KNOW

"ALL I KNOW IS THAT I KNOW NOTHING."

— SOCRATES

When we first begin dancing, we are at Stage 1: We don't know what we don't know. Dancing is fun, though we have little understanding of steps, dance styles, postures, or arm styling. We dance because it makes us laugh and feel connected; it enables us to meet other people. **We don't know what we don't know and we don't care!** We let our instructors, friends, and dance partners lead us through the basic steps with little or no resistance. We feel free to express our joys and dance with a carefree attitude.

When I first started dancing, I remember having fun and laughing at my feeble attempts to get the basic merengue steps and pace working simultaneously. I was thrilled just to move my feet in the same direction, and my instructor was encouraging and kind. I looked forward to each lesson and couldn't wait to put on my dance shoes and be part of this exhilarating community. It wasn't only about the actual dancing at this stage; it was also about the people I met at the studio, the excitement of entering into a world where I was a novice, where I had to give up control and let my instructor take charge. For someone like me who is hired to lead and teach others to do the same, learning to follow was a completely new experience.

Stage 1, which can last for a few lessons or for a couple of months, is **characterized by fun, fearlessness, positive energy, laughing, and excitement.**

After a while, most dancers begin to ask for more information from their instructors and want to learn advanced steps and techniques. They may observe other dancers and seek to emulate a specific move or another's style. At this point, we move into Stage 2.

STAGE 2 / CONSCIOUS INCOMPETENCE: WE KNOW THAT WE DON'T KNOW

"YOU ARE STILL TAKING DANCE LESSONS? HAVEN'T YOU LEARNED IT BY NOW? AT SOME POINT EACH OF US DISCOVERS THAT DANCING IS A RECEDING HORIZON. THERE IS NO POINT AT WHICH WE HAVE FINISHED LEARNING."

— ELIZABETH AND ARTHUR SEAGULL, AUTHORS OF *BALLROOM DANCING IS NOT FOR SISSIES*

As we slowly realize how much we don't know about dancing, some of the fun and excitement wears off. We begin to recognize nuances and understand that, in addition to the basic steps, we also need to master hip movements, body rhythms, and floor crafting. With this newfound knowledge, we can **feel a bit deflated or unmotivated.** We reflect back to when we started and are aware that we had no clue what we were doing. We might beat up on ourselves for looking silly or like a novice.

For me, this stage became apparent when I started to compare myself to other dancers. I remember asking my instructor how long they had been dancing, why they were styling their arms and I wasn't, and I realized that Cuban motion was not the same as wiggling my hips back and forth (one of my instructor's pet peeves). All of a sudden, I saw that I had A LOT to learn, and I began to feel **insecure, inadequate, and afraid of appearing foolish.**

If these sentiments resonate with you as you ponder moving forward with your dancing, know that they are perfectly normal and actually helpful, as you will discover later in this book. After all, you are reading this book because you are contemplating or are ready for advancing, and the only way to do so is to go through Stage 2. While Stage 1 feels good, getting through Stage 2 will allow you to be good.

STAGE 3 / CONSCIOUS COMPETENCE: WE KNOW THAT WE KNOW

"I DO NOT TRY TO DANCE BETTER THAN ANYONE ELSE. I ONLY TRY TO DANCE BETTER THAN MYSELF."

— MIKHAIL BARYSHNIKOV

Once we get through our "challenging" feelings and improve our skills, attitudes, and competence, we realize that pushing through Stage 2 enabled us to experience **deep joy, accomplishment, and a sense of pride.** We have developed conscious competence: We know that we know what we are doing. We may say things like: "I made a mistake in my rumba walks, and I'll work on improving that," or "I know that posture is one of the most important aspects judges look at in competitions." It doesn't necessarily mean that we have perfected or mastered the steps or techniques, but at this stage we know the difference. **This is where the fun continues!** We can fine-tune, practice, and add more advanced steps to our repertoires. With each new accomplishment, our confidence grows.

I clearly remember the day when my coach approached me to correct my posture (for the hundredth time) in the waltz, and I auto-corrected before she was able to reach me. I felt proud of all the hard work and commitment I had put in to making that small change.

STAGE 4 / UNCONSCIOUS COMPETENCE: IT'S SECOND NATURE

"WE BECOME WHAT WE REPEATEDLY DO. EXCELLENCE THEN, IS NOT AN ACT BUT A HABIT."

— ARISTOTLE

Most of us linger in Stage 3 for a long time. We may even find that for certain dances or techniques, we remain in Stage 3 for months or years. There is nothing wrong with that. But in some dance styles we are able to push through to Stage 4; Unconscious Competence, where the steps and techniques have become second nature. Professional dancers rarely think about the basic techniques as they teach or perform. They know them by heart. That doesn't mean that they don't have to work hard on perfecting each move or step, and if you have ever watched a professional dancer practice, you know this is true. The difference is that they no longer have to think about why they do what they do. They can work with coaches who offer specific feedback and adjust their moves quickly and gain immediate results. Depending on your current level of dancing, you may find that you now do your Bronze I and II steps with unconscious competence, or that you no longer have to think about the alignments or foot positions to execute the steps. For other levels, you may still be at stages 1, 2, or 3.

Stage 4 usually brings a variety of emotions and feelings. While we may still feel **excited, proud, and accomplished, we can also become judgmental, frustrated, or annoyed** if we can't learn something new as quickly as we would like or if we make basic mistakes. While this stage is complex, it tends to be **less confusing or frustrating than earlier stages**. Here, we know what we know and we know what we don't know, and we have learned to maximize our best assets. We have also been through stages 1, 2, and 3, and we have become more familiar with the Stages of Change. Many dancers who reach Stage 4 have started to compete and enjoy the feedback and rewards that come from being judged and challenged.

I remember practicing by myself at the studio, and at some point I looked up in the mirror and realized that my upper body seemed to finally know how to connect to the rest of my body. I had worked so hard on trying to make my body "get it," and it seemed that it would never happen. But through tenacious repetition, my body had finally converted the process in to muscle memory. Much of dancing technique is simply repetition, repetition, repetition—of the correct movements, of course.

SELF-REFLECTIVE EXERCISE:

→ After reviewing the four Stages of Change, circle the stage you currently identify most with:

STAGE 1 / UNCONSCIOUS INCOMPETENCE: I DON'T KNOW WHAT I DON'T KNOW

STAGE 2 / CONSCIOUS INCOMPETENCE: I KNOW WHAT I DON'T KNOW

STAGE 3 / CONSCIOUS COMPETENCE: I KNOW WHAT I KNOW

STAGE 4 / UNCONSCIOUS COMPETENCE: IT'S SECOND NATURE

→ What are the benefits of being at this stage in your dancing?

_____

_____

_____

→ What are the challenges of being at this stage in your dancing?

_____

_____

_____

→ What do you need to change, shift, or modify to take your dancing to the next level?

_____

_____

_____

EXPERT ADVICE:

BONITA BROCKERT WAS A THREE-TIME U.S. FINALIST IN THE INTERNATIONAL TOUR OF "DANCING NIGHTS." SHE IS A NATIONAL JUDGE, CHOREOGRAPHER, AND COACH IN CINCINNATI, OHIO.

JF: You are an experienced competitive dancer and master coach to hundreds of amateurs and professionals. At what stage in a dancer's training do they tend to seek your help?

BONITA: *I work with dancers at all these levels, although sometimes they may be at one place with some of their skills and in a completely different place with others. I don't think there is one particular pattern to this.*

JF: What advice do you have for dancers in stages 2, 3, and 4 to help them break through to the next level in their dancing?

BONITA: *First, realize that for as long as you dance or perform you're moving through these levels in some way, in some aspect of your skill set. Whether changing venues—for instance, ballroom to stage—or starting with a new partner, learning new choreography or dance style, or creating new movements, dancers progress through these stages.*

It is also important to understand what Stage 4 is. Don't expect things to happen without focus and proper attention and awareness. All top performers, pros included, have "off nights" or bad games. "The foundation of 'unconscious acting' is awareness," says Darryl Hickman, in The Unconscious Actor: Out of Control, In Full Command. Substitute dancing or tennis or any other endeavor for acting, and this thought will carry a lot of weight.

You can never take your performance for granted! Of course, your training base will support you, provided that you have established it adequately! But you have to stay focused no matter where you are in your technique and performance journey. The "second nature" or "muscle memory," your ability to FEEL your technique and to articulate multiple elements in your movement, is the bank you draw from. But your focus, awareness, in-the-moment presence must be switched on!

To move from one plateau to the next, you need the right coach who will know not only how to help you through proper body mechanics, but also knows what needs to be addressed and when. Many things correct themselves as you go, and knowing what to focus on at what time is crucial to avoiding the "stuck" place, which is so frustrating. Many dancers try to emulate a "look" or product, not understanding that the process and understanding of mechanics and musicality will eventually produce the right look. When you build from the inside out, with lengthening instead of tensing, structure without rigidity, prioritizing fundamentals and giving the work the time and respect required, you will achieve lasting results and the confidence that comes from real integrity over forced positions and rigid attempts to produce a certain look.

Remember also that we have a syllabus for a very good reason. So many times I hear students say that Bronze or Silver is boring. You may want to dance pivots before you can walk, or dance open Latin before you can produce a respectable fan, but you will not get very far if you to follow that path. There are no shortcuts to good dancing and, in the long run, if you put the cart before the horse, you will have a long row to hoe when you finally realize how many poor habits are formed on such diversions! Also, the importance of small successes along the way boost confidence and feed your desire to do better. So dance in your appropriate category, give yourself the opportunity to grow within that level, then move on! Be sure you are fully prepared for showcases or other "under fire" situations.

A note to professionals is to remember to plan your rest times! This was certainly a failing of mine when I was dancing 10 dances. The more dances you have to rehearse, the more likely you are to make this mistake. Dancers tend to be distrustful of their training base and feel that they will "lose it" if they dare to take a day off, let alone two! Many of us are obsessive—we prefer to call it passionate!—and have to be as disciplined with time off as we are with practice time. The fields of dance and sports medicine have made great strides in the past ten years, and one important element now stressed is the planned rest time so that you can peak for your performance, rather than two days later or earlier. Rest is also crucial to injury prevention, to the health of your partnership, and to allow your neurological system to process skill and information. Balance is a good goal for training freaks to add to their plate!

While reflecting on and thinking about your dancing will help you better understand yourself, it will not actually change anything on a tactical level; however, your action steps will.

Each section in this book has an **"Action Step"** exercise that includes a **dancing tip** and a **coaching tip**. The dancing tips are practical and ready-to-implement strategies that will help your dancing improve. The coaching tips are meant to challenge your thinking and help you to process your emotions about the changes you are making on a holistic level. **Remember: who you are on the dance floor is most likely a direct reflection of who you are off the dance floor.** As you will come to see, developing your dancing skills will allow you to develop as a person as well.

The final part is an action statement or what we call an **"I will" statement**. Nothing will change unless you do something differently. The "I will" statements—as opposed to "I may" or "I'll think about" statements, which are not action focused—should be small and measurable. Big, sweeping statements tend to overwhelm us and rarely produce the actions we hope for. There are plenty of action step exercises in this book, so keep your commitments concise. When you add them together, they will produce significant results.

In Chapter 8 you will find a summary and list of action steps by chapter. It may be helpful to review this periodically as you work through each chapter.

ACTION STEP

DANCING TIP 1 / Set aside 15-20 minutes of uninterrupted time to review your current dancing stage. Take out a notebook or piece of paper and write down the emotions you feel—positive and negative—about being at this stage. Review your notes and write an action statement that will help you embrace your stage. For example, you may write: "It's okay for me to feel insecure and unsure right now. I recognize that these are natural emotions connected to this stage. The next time I feel this way, I will remind myself that it is perfectly normal and I won't let the feelings affect my dancing." Or, "Right now, I'm feeling 'in the groove' about my Swing and will enjoy this moment for as long as it lasts." The idea behind this action step is to increase your self-awareness about your prevailing dancing stage and avoid making judgments about it. What keeps most of us from moving forward with our dancing is not our technical or physical ability. Instead, it is the "head trash" we carry around in our minds that stops us dead in our tracks. Use this exercise or action statement to develop your self-awareness.

COACHING TIP 1 / Set aside 15-20 minutes of uninterrupted time and take out a notebook or piece of paper. List at least three areas of your life, besides dancing, where the stages apply, such as work, intimate relationships, friendships, or other hobbies. For each of the areas, assign your current stage, noting 1-4 next to each. It could be that you are struggling to break through to the next level in a personal relationship and list it at Stage 2. Or you may be in the groove in your new business and list it at Stage 1. It could be that your friendships are solid and developed and they are at Stage 4. When you are done, review your list and see if there is a common thread between the areas in your life and your dancing. Look for patterns of behavior or thinking that may help or hurt you at each stage. For those areas you wish to change, list one small action step you can take to move it to the next level.

"I WILL...."

GETTING THROUGH

CHAPTER 2:

STAGE 2
—THE FIRST TIME

"IN CONFRONTING YOUR FEARS OF INADEQUACY, INCOMPETENCE, UNDESERVINGNESS, CAN YOU BEAR THE POSSIBILITY OF SMASHING THE DREAM? CAN YOU BEAR FAILURE? THESE ARE THE QUESTIONS I ASKED MYSELF, AND I KNEW **MY DESIRE TO DANCE WAS SO POWERFUL** THAT I WOULD RISK IT."

— LYDIA RAURELL, AUTHOR OF *A YEAR OF DANCING DANGEROUSLY*

Stage 1 is a positive and exciting experience, and we don't need a whole lot of help moving through it. We most definitely need help with Stage 2. This is when we begin to feel insecure, unmotivated, and frustrated. It is also when our "dark sides" tend to appear, when we are prone to judge ourselves and others and make excuses for a lack of progress. I know from experience. It doesn't sound good, but the most important point is that you are reading this book and so recognize that **you need help and support to take yourself gracefully through this stage.** If you identified most with Stage 2 in the previous chapter, the next couple of pages will help you move through this stage with increased confidence, energy, and determination. As the heading implies, you may as well get really good at it, as you will go through Stage 2 over and over again as you develop your dancing.

STEP 1 / RECONNECTING WITH YOUR DANCE PASSION

"DANCING IS MY OBSESSION. MY LIFE."

— MIKHAIL BARYSHNIKOV

When you first started dancing and enjoyed the bliss of Stage 1, you probably felt joy and excitement while dancing. As you enter Stage 2 and experience fear, self-doubt, and self-criticism, it's important to reconnect with the positive feelings and emotions of Stage 1 and **recall why you love to dance in the first place.** As you will discover in this book, most amateur and professional dancers have to remind themselves constantly why they love to dance to maintain their focus, foster their passion, and push themselves to higher achievement.

If taking your dancing to the next level includes competing or performing, Stage 2 is a key portal that will require you to move outside of your comfort zone. Even for the most ambitious and risk-embracing person, these challenges can cause discomfort and doubt. These are natural feelings that you will need to push through. Reconnecting to the wonderful benefits dancing has brought to your life will help propel you to new heights of personal satisfaction.

SELF-REFLECTIVE EXERCISE:

1. Recall the moment you were introduced to ballroom dancing, and you connected with your passion or love for dancing / List at least three positive and three challenging feelings evoked by that experience. Remember that having both "good" and "bad" feelings is normal. If you can't recall the first time, think back to a time when you knew you wanted to continue dancing because it offered you something important.

POSITIVE FEELINGS	CHALLENGING FEELINGS
I felt...	I felt...
1.	1.
2.	2.
3.	3.
4.	4.

2. Pick one response from the "positive feeling" / list that connects closest to your heart at this time and write it in the space below. This is the feeling I want you to recall whenever you are especially tested in your dancing. It may be helpful to ask yourself why you love to dance in the first place to find this answer.

3. Pick one response from the "challenging feeling" / list that is most likely to derail you and record it in the space below. This is usually a feeling connected to your deepest vulnerability or insecurity.

This exercise is meant to help you reconnect with your passion for dancing and remind you of positive feelings when going through Stage 2. It is also meant to shed light on your most challenging feelings so that you can acknowledge them without letting them stand in your way.

EXPERT ADVICE:

PAMELA BOLLING WAS THE 2008 AND 2009 OHIO STAR BALL PRO/AM 9-DANCE WORLD CHAMPION AND THE 2010 AMERICAN SMOOTH PRO/AM U.S. CHAMPION. SHE LIVES IN ORLANDO, FLA.

JF: You are one of the top U.S. amateur competitors and an accomplished ballet, jazz, and contemporary dancer and choreographer. How did you discover ballroom dancing, and what has propelled you forward so quickly?

PAMELA: *I was approaching my late 30s and was faced with several personal losses in close succession. It made me stop and consider the short time we all have in this life. I had already had great success as a dancer but always felt like I had missed out on experiencing ballroom dancing. The timing seemed perfect, and as soon as I took a few lessons, I knew I had found a missing piece. It wasn't just the dancing itself that hooked me. I was edging closer to 40 and needed to keep exercising to stay in shape. Hitting the treadmill just wasn't my thing. Ballroom dancing fulfilled my need for fun exercise, mental stimulation, and emotional stamina.*

Because I'm a consummate learner and am internally driven to challenge myself, I dove into ballroom head first. After a few months, my instructor asked if I wanted to do a ballroom competition, and I thought, why not? I had no idea what to expect. Hotlanta Dance Challenge was our first competition, and we did extremely well. That experience sparked a true passion for ballroom dancing in me, and I realized how much I still had to learn. I decided to go all out. I began with a few lessons a week, and very shortly thereafter found myself dancing several days a week and doubling up on my lessons.

After a few months I recognized that if I was going to hit my dancing goals, I needed to gain more competition experience. I signed up for one or two competitions per month and for over a year. I danced all over the United States and gained invaluable experience about competing, dance techniques, judging, and costuming. My internally competitive spark kept me pushing forward.

What I didn't realize then was how much I would enjoy the camaraderie of dancing and competing. Now, that is almost as important to me as performing well and pushing myself to the next level. I realize that I dance because I love dancing but also because I love people. Dancing is a fun, positive, and energizing sport. It requires a lot of dedication, determination, and stamina. I think it attracts people who like to compete but also those who enjoy doing it with other people. In what other sport can you get dressed up in amazing costumes, get your hair and makeup done, and hang out with your girlfriends? This is a sport where being "girly" and getting dressed up are appreciated and valued.

JF: What tips would you share with dancers who want to take their dancing to the next level but are experiencing Stage 2 for the first time and may be feeling insecurity, fear, or self-doubt?

PAMELA: You have to remind yourself why you love to dance in the first place. For me, it comes down to having fun and constantly learning something new. I have to remember that I am not a professional ballroom dancer and that this is my hobby. It may be a passion, but it is still something I do because I choose to. If it stops being fun, I will stop doing it. It's that simple.

When I first started competing, my instructor and I had great success. We just had fun and enjoyed our unexpected accomplishments. I guess that is what you call Stage 1; we didn't know what we didn't know and we didn't care. As I danced and competed more, I realized how much I didn't know, and I had to go through Stage 2 and felt insecure and overwhelmed. I think these powerful feelings stop people from pushing through and reaching their goals. The truth is that we all go through them. Those are the times when you just have to stay with it and remember how much fun you had the first time dancing came into your life. I love Winston Churchill's quotation:

"Never give in, never give in, never; never; never; never—in nothing, great or small, large or petty—never give in except to convictions of honor and good sense." If you can't remember how to put the fun back in to your dancing, ask someone who can. Ask yourself questions like, "Why am I not having as much fun as I used to?" or "What was I doing when I was having fun dancing?" Chances are that you will find your way back.

If you want to continue to dance, you have to look internally for motivation and not worry about what other people think of you. It is easy to get caught up in trying to please other people, but the truth is that the only person who has to be happy with your dancing is you. If I find myself getting caught up in what judges may think of my dancing, I remember that "people judge and judges are people." I recognize that I can write my own script and decide how I am going to feel and act to make myself happy.

ACTION STEP

DANCING TIP 2 / If you carry a dancing notebook or dance bag, record the positive and challenging feeling you listed above and take it with you as you dance and practice. If your motivation goes down and you feel discouraged or insecure, review the positive feeling. If you begin to question yourself and your decision to take on this new initiative, review the challenging feeling and remember that having gotten past it initially got you to where you are today. By continuing to push through, you will reach your goals and achieve the next level of performance.

COACHING TIP 2 / Be kind to yourself and remember that in other parts of your life, you have gone through Stage 2 several times and have emerged a better person. Think of a time in your life, outside of dancing, when you went through a particularly challenging Stage 2. List at least five characteristics, behaviors, or actions that helped you get through it. Review your list and see if any of these strategies apply to your feelings and emotions at Stage 2 in your dancing. You may discover that asking for help or staying positive in the face of adversity are your greatest strengths. Applying them to your dancing will likely produce faster and more rewarding results. As the ancient philosopher Confucius said, "Wherever you go, there you are." Simply changing your environment isn't going to give you different outcomes. Changing the way you think and act will.

"I WILL…."

STEP 2 / CONDUCT A SKILLS AND ATTITUDE AUDIT

"IF YOU DON'T LIKE SOMETHING, CHANGE IT. IF YOU CAN'T CHANGE IT, **CHANGE YOUR ATTITUDE.**"

— MAYA ANGELOU

Now that you have connected with your passion for dance, let's look at your dance skills and attitudes. Later in this book we will dig a little deeper in to your specific strengths and weaknesses. Begin now by thinking about attributes and outlooks you possess that can help or hurt your dancing. Being a good dancer requires natural talent and hard work. **Being a great dancer involves sharpening your skills and maintaining an unfalteringly positive frame of mind.**

My favorite business guru is Jim Collins, author of *Good to Great*. In 2001 I had the privilege of hearing him speak. The first thing out of his mouth was, "Good is the enemy of great," which has been a central principle for me ever since. If we settle for good, we will never experience how great we can be. Taking yourself from good to great requires effort and commitment. It also demands a willingness to look, in a brutally honest way, at your strengths and weaknesses.

Before deciding what the next steps may be in your dancing, let's conduct an initial skills and attitude audit.

SELF-REFLECTIVE EXERCISE:

1. What dancing skill are you most proud of?

_____

_____

_____

2. What dancing flaw are you most sensitive about?

_____

_____

_____

3. What dancing skills do you need to work on to take your dancing to the next level?

_____

_____

_____

4. What are you willing to do or invest to take yourself there?

_____

_____

_____

5. If you could change one thing about your own attitude regarding Stage 2 to become more positive about your dancing, what would it be?

_____

_____

6. Circle one positive affirmation statement on the next page that you will begin using to embrace your dancing, dance level, and stage. If none of the options fit, please write your own statement below:

_____

_____

_____

- I completely and fully embrace my dancing where I am right now.
- I love to dance; it brings me joy.
- I am a wonderful dancer because I love to dance.
- I love to dance, and others notice how much I enjoy it.
- Dancing brings me happiness.
- I'm exactly where I need to be in my dancing right now.
- I can always improve as a dancer, and I embrace my current stage.
- I dance because I love it.
- My love for dance is enough.
- Dancing fulfills me.
- When I dance, I'm completely present; I'm doing what I love.
- I allow myself to be vulnerable when I dance.
- Growing as a dancer is scary, but I choose to do it anyway.
- (insert your own below.)

_____

_____

Positive affirmations help us stay connected to and honest about our dancing. The truth is that even the most successful dancers go through Stage 2, and they make a conscious decision to hone their skills and keep their attitudes in check. Beginner, intermediate, and advanced dancers need to do the same.

EXPERT ADVICE:

BILL SPARKS IS A FOUR-TIME U.S. LATIN CHAMPION. HE IS AN ADJUDICATOR AND PREMIER COACH IN COLUMBUS, OHIO

JF: You are a champion dancer and coach to top professionals all over the country. To what one skill or habit do you attribute your success as a competitive dancer? Looking back to when you danced competitively, what attitude or skill do you wish you had known about earlier to make yourself even more successful?

BILL: *Although I could come up with a series of different attributes that contributed to my success, it all boils down to consistent hard work. But it's not just about working hard. You have to be persistently goal focused and want to pursue excellence. For me, repetition was the key. I pushed myself because I always knew that I could do more and be better. Being just "good" wasn't enough.*

Looking back, I wish I had been a bit more open to listening and following my dance partners. It would have enabled me to gain complementary knowledge and skills that I may have shut out by being overly focused on my own process. I could have been more empathetic and open to my coaches' feedback. Dancing is a high-energy sport, and it pushes your emotions and feelings. I wish I had focused less on my feelings and more on incorporating the advice others were giving me.

JF: What tips would you share with dancers who are experiencing Stage 2 for the first time to help them get through it faster and with more confidence?

BILL: *Go back to and re-analyze what you are doing. Review your routines or choreography to see where you can break through. Listen to music to rediscover your strengths. Increase your knowledge in any way you can. Educate yourself. It's a long process.*

ACTION STEP

DANCING TIP 3 / Write your positive affirmation statement and keep it in a place where you see it every day—maybe a Post-It note in your car, a screen-saver on your computer, or a picture on your phone that provides a visual memory cue. The key is to look at the statement daily and reaffirm the positive thoughts you need to motivate yourself and boost your dancing. You may even want to share it with your instructor so that he or she can support your growth and development.

COACHING TIP 3 / Make a list of at least 10 skills, characteristics, or talents that you possess. It may be that you are generous, a good listener, supportive of others, an initiator, or willing to challenge yourself and others. Think of what makes you unique. Review the list and draw parallels to your dancing. Are you a great student because you listen to your instructor? Have you advanced quicker than others because you constantly challenge yourself?

Next, review the list and see if any of your strengths can be overextended and, therefore, hurt your dancing. It may be that you are so supportive of others that you don't have enough time for yourself and your dance practice. Or, it may be that you are so determined and self-motivated that you forget to listen to others who can help you develop. Any strength when overused becomes a weakness. The challenge is to balance your strengths to gain the most from them.

"I WILL...."

GETTING THROUGH STAGE 2
— OVER

CHAPTER 3:

AND OVER AND OVER AGAIN

"TWENTY YEARS FROM NOW YOU WILL BE MORE DISAPPOINTED BY THE THINGS YOU DIDN'T DO THAN BY THE ONES YOU DID DO. SO THROW OFF THE BOWLINES. SAIL AWAY FROM THE SAFE HARBOR. CATCH THE TRADE WINDS IN YOUR SAILS. EXPLORE. DREAM. DISCOVER."

— MARK TWAIN

Okay, so the truth is that you will go through Stage 2 over and over and over and over again! All dancers do. It is easy to give up at this stage, walk away from dancing, and never look back. Some people do. It takes courage, tenacity, and faith to go through Stage 2 over and over again, and it's not for everyone. The fact that you are still dancing and reading this book tells me that you have the stamina and determination to make it through to the next level of your dancing. Stage 2 is here to stay and so are many of the emotions that come with the pain of growing and developing. I find this quote by Dan Millman, author of Body Mind Mastery, to be especially helpful to avoid getting stuck in the negative emotions that come with Stage 2:

"**Acknowledging an emotional obstruction**—'I'm afraid,' 'I feel angry' —seems essential for optimal health. **But obsessing** about fear, habitually dramatizing it, and struggling to find it only reinforces the obstruction. Instead, pay attention to doing whatever you are doing with elegance."

When we move into new steps, decide to go from bronze to silver, or learn different dances, we have to go through Stage 2 all over again. You may even go through Stage 2 after correcting a specific technique within a step or dance. While it may be painful at times, that is what makes dancing such an exciting sport. And the more you practice the exercises in this book, the faster you will move through your Stage 2 experiences and the closer you will get to your dancing goals.

STEP 1 / REMIND YOURSELF THAT YOU'VE BEEN HERE BEFORE AND WILL BE AGAIN!

"I CAN DO THIS, BUT IT'S GOING TO BE HARD. I CAN GET THROUGH THIS BECAUSE I HAVE THE SCARS TO PROVE I HAVE BEFORE."

— TEMPLETON THOMPSON

I love the song **"I Can Do This"** by Templeton Thompson, which goes: "I can do this, but it's going to be hard. I can get through this because I have the scars to prove I have before." For me, going through Stage 2 for the first time was far harder than the hundred times I have gone through it since. At least now I know what to expect and I have the tools to move along. Dancing requires a certain set of physical skills, but more importantly, it is absolutely essential that you know how to master your thinking. As you will learn in this book, the most influential person on your dancing journey is you. You hold the key to your success and advancement, and the better you get at moving through Stage 2, the more time and energy you can spend actually dancing.

SELF-REFLECTIVE EXERCISE:

1. What do you need to do or tell yourself to remember that you've been here before?

_____

_____

_____

_____

2. Who will you call or connect with to remind you when you lose sight of the fact that you've been here before and you got through it? (Instructors, coaches, and close dance friends are great accountability partners.)

_____

_____

_____

_____

EXPERT ADVICE

MAUREEN ANDREWS IS A PRO/AM COMPETITOR IN COLUMBUS, OHIO.

JF: You have successfully competed in Pro/Am for more than 10 years, and you dance all four styles (Latin, Rhythm, Smooth, and Standard). What do you do or tell yourself to avoid being frustrated or having self-limiting beliefs?

MAUREEN: *I ask myself three key questions to make sure I am on the right path as I dance and compete.*

First, do I have excellent communication or am I willing to invest in being an excellent communicator with my pro? If you can't communicate well and often with your partner, you create unnecessary tension and stress, which will negatively affect your dancing. I continuously check with my partner to make sure we are seeing eye to eye. The communication allows me to better understand the dance movement and to fully respond to my partner's lead.

Second, I ask myself, do I trust my partner's experience, expertise, and advice? Every pro teaches, communicates, and interacts in different ways. To take my dancing to the next level, I need to trust that my partner has my best interest at heart and that he has the abilities and experience to help me reach my goals. It is also important to recognize that we, as amateurs, may not always be ready to hear what our pros are telling us at a particular moment, especially if they are pushing us outside of our comfort zones. We may have to hear the same message over and over again until we can absorb the feedback. Remember that the Pro/Am relationship goes both ways.

Third, I remind myself that this is a hobby. Am I having fun? Am I growing the way I want to? There have been times when I've compared my dancing to that of female pros, and I have to remind myself that this isn't my career. Comparing myself to a standard that requires a completely different commitment than I am willing to make will not help me become a better dancer. Instead, I watch the pros and pick up on techniques and movements that I, with my pro's help, want to incorporate or emulate. I find that going to competitions helps me get a visual representation of what I want to incorporate in to my dancing as I grow and develop.

JF: If you could offer dancers at Stage 2 one tip about how to move through this stage repeatedly, what would it be?

MAUREEN: *Build a network of female amateur dancers. Talk to other students to get support, encouragement, and feedback. I go through Stage 2 all the time, and each time I ask myself if this is something I want to continue doing. Growing as a dancer can be painful, and it is challenging. Luckily, the answer is always yes for me, and it has been for more than 10 years. We all experience meltdowns as we grow. When you have a support network and you love to dance, it is a lot easier to get through the challenging times.*

ACTION STEP

DANCING TIP 4 / Connect with a dancing friend and grab lunch or coffee. Share thoughts and scenarios about how you get through Stage 2 and develop strategies for supporting each other in the future. Remember that your fellow dancers are experiencing many of the same things you are. By networking and connecting with them, you will find strength and encouragement to help you through challenging times, and you will likely build lifelong friendships.

COACHING TIP 4 / Find a favorite song, quote, poem, or saying that reminds you that you've been here before (and will be again) to help you through this stage faster and without leaving bruises. I keep a playlist on my iPhone with "feel good" songs that I play when I need added encouragement. Some of my favorite songs include "I Can Do This" by Templeton Thompson, "Come as You Are" by Jaci Velasquez, and "Turn It Over" by Leslie Mendelson. Each song gives me a different version of the same feeling—the feeling that I have what it takes to go through this again by just being myself.

"I WILL...."

STEP 2 / CONTROL YOUR GREMLINS!

"WE CANNOT CHANGE ANYTHING UNTIL WE ACCEPT IT."

— CARL JUNG

In Gremlins, a movie popular from 1984, a young boy inadvertently breaks the rules while caring for his unusual pet and unintentionally unleashes a horde of hideous monsters. They wreak havoc and set out to destroy anything that gets in their way. What initially look like cuddly little pets turn out to be nasty, devious, harmful monsters.

We will use the gremlins analogy as visual representations of our most invasive fears. While fears can sometimes protect us from getting hurt and serve as early warning signals to keep us from making mistakes, they can also limit our abilities to push through a difficult situation and stunt our growth. **We all have little gremlins that "protect" us from doing things that may be uncomfortable or make us look foolish.** They live in the back of our minds and won't go away easily, if ever. So what we have to do is control them so they don't interfere or hinder our dancing progress. Successful dancers acknowledge them, firmly tell them to take a nap, and move right along despite their anxiety.

Gremlins are usually based in some sort of truth. For me, a recurring gremlin that I carry around is that I'm a slow learner. When I reflect honestly, I admit to the fact that I need a lot of time, repetition, and practice to learn something new. The gremlin part of my self-limiting belief is that *I should* catch on faster, and that part of the statement beats me up unnecessarily. I have learned to replace the second part with a new conclusion: I'm a slow learner, and I need to practice hard to catch up to those who learn faster. All of a sudden, the fact that I learn slowly is okay. My strategy is to work harder and practice more, which makes me a better dancer. Every time I remind myself of the true statement, the little gremlin in my head pouts but then backs off. Too bad for it! I'm not willing to let a little furry monster hold me back from being the dancer of my dreams!

So bring out your gremlins, and let's design counterstrategies to help you take your dancing one step further.

SELF-REFLECTIVE EXERCISE:

1. Write down what your most aggressive and destructive gremlin would say about your dancing.

2. What part of that statement is true or has some truth to it?

3. Which part is holding you back?

4. How would you change the statement to acknowledge what is true about it and change the ending to serve you and your dancing goals?

EXPERT ADVICE:

IZABELLA JUNDZILL WAS A NATIONAL FINALIST IN THE PROFESSIONAL AMERICAN SMOOTH. SHE IS AN INSTRUCTOR, ADJUDICATOR, AND COACH IN WILMINGTON, DEL.

JF: You are a national finalist professional smooth dancer and a Pro/Am teacher. What is one of your most destructive gremlins, and how have you learned to push through in spite of it?

IZABELLA: *My most destructive gremlin is the "self-doubter." It's the little voice in the back of my head that says, "You can't do it. Are you sure you are good enough?" It sneaks up on me before every competition, and I have learned to listen to, acknowledge, and appreciate it. It is what fuels me to push through my fears to reach the next level. Everyone has gremlins, and they just look different to different people. The key is to ask yourself if you are ready to face them. Trying to avoid them or pretending they aren't there will only make them appear stronger. I listen to my gremlins and try to understand why these thoughts are coming to me. Most of us dance for a reason. I believe that, in addition to wanting to have fun and challenge ourselves, we dance to confront certain fears or insecurities. We may want to overcome our shyness, or become more in touch with our bodies, emotions, and physical boundaries. Or we may want to prove to ourselves and others that we can accomplish something challenging. The very reasons we are attracted to dancing and competing may be directly linked to our most pervasive gremlins. So, learning to manage them becomes a constant and imperative part of the dancing process.*

When you compete, you have to remember that you are not in control of the judges, other dancers, or the environment. All you have control of is your own thinking and emotions. You have to learn to believe in yourself. This is much easier said than done, but you have to start now and get really good at it if you want to take your dancing to the next level. While it is essential to have a network of supportive people around you who believe in you, you can't rely on them to take care of you emotionally.

That job is yours. When you are in the on-deck area or about to go out on stage to do a show dance, the only person you have is YOU.

Because our gremlins tend to appear when we are most vulnerable, we have to practice getting ready before it's too late. Practice and patience are the keys to overcoming gremlins. Use positive affirmation statements or key words to combat your self-defeating thinking. Even if you don't yet believe in them, keep saying them over and over again. The more you repeat them, the more you will believe them. The short of it is that you can't worry about pleasing other people. The only person you need to please is yourself. I personally feel like I win every time I have met my own professional goals.

JF: *What tips would you share with dancers who are experiencing Stage 2 again and may feel like their own self-limiting beliefs or gremlins are holding them back?*

IZABELLA: *Figure out one thing that you do really well or better than most other people. Consider all aspects of your life when identifying your unique gifts. What motivates us in life tends to be what motivates us to dance. Then consider how you can incorporate your strengths into your dancing. If you find this challenging, you may want to ask someone who knows you well to share what you are really great at.*

The other thing is to ask questions to widen your perspective. Dancers have to be extremely self-aware. They have to constantly check in with their mental, physical, and emotional centers. I often ask myself, "Am I in good shape? Where is my mental state? What else do I need to feel fulfilled?"

ACTION STEP:

DANCING TIP 5 / Share your gremlin or self-limiting belief with your instructor and tell him or her how to help you move through it. Remember to be specific and share when and how you prefer to receive the feedback. You may want to come up with a specific cue that reminds both of you that the gremlin is about to rear its ugly head or has already appeared. This exercise will help you and your instructor bond and will eliminate unnecessary communication challenges.

COACHING TIP 5 / Set aside 30 minutes of uninterrupted time. Pick one gremlin that seems to show up in your life on a constant basis.

A gremlin of mine is that I'm not smart enough. On paper, it doesn't make much sense, as I have advanced degrees, own a business, and am successful at most things I put my mind to. But deep down inside me is that little gremlin that shows up no matter how many degrees or awards I receive.

Consider your gremlin. Where do you think it comes from? What is your earliest memory of where that programming may have come from? Did you get critical feedback from someone when you were young? Most gremlins are rooted in an experience or a set of experiences that made you believe these self-defeating statements early in life. Once you have identified one or several sources, write down what the adult, self-confident version of you would say or do in that particular scenario. For me, it's not a specific person or event that comes to mind. Instead, it is the lack of feedback I received as a young child about my accomplishments. No one was there to challenge me or to give me positive feedback, so I always wondered if what I felt or thought was true. As an adult, I remind myself and my gremlin that I am smart enough. It may sound simple, but that doesn't mean it is easy.

"I WILL...."

CHAPTER THREE / THE BALLROOM DANCE COACH

STEP 3 / LISTEN TO YOUR INNER COACH

"HE WHO LOOKS OUTSIDE, DREAMS; WHO LOOKS INSIDE, AWAKENS."

— CARL JUNG

My job is to coach business leaders to produce extraordinary results. I know from personal and professional experience that working with an objective external adviser helps you to see yourself and your abilities from a different perspective. I couldn't have built the business I have today without the support and critical feedback of my coaches.

But it wasn't until I read Lydia Raurell's book, *A Year of Dancing Dangerously*, that I connected with the concept of having my own "inner coach" on and off the dance floor. Like many ballroom dancers, Lydia fell head over heals in love with ballroom dancing and competing. What is unusual about her is that she decided to push herself to her utmost limit. Through a year of committing all of her energy, time, and passion to her dancing, she earned the title "top student" at the prestigious Ohio Star Ball. This accomplishment is truly admirable. To achieve it, Lydia had to compete in six regions and dance for more than 22 days in a three-month period and then repeat that process over and over again. She also had to dance an impressive amount of heats in each competition and place in the top spots to reach this goal. Here is how she describes relying on her inner coach to push through the ever-repeating Stage 2:

> *My inner coach is very persuasive, though; in fact, somewhat to my surprise, she is quite formidable. More than anything she hates to give up. During my worst moments of fear and anxiety, my inner coach pushes her way to the front of my mind, reminds me of the promise I made to myself, and coaxes me through the steps. We work them together, my inner coach and I, perhaps a little obsessively, until they are smooth, and I have remembered that I am a Dancer.*

I recall practicing alone at the dance studio. I was getting frustrated and angry with myself for not getting a certain move, when our amazing studio owner, Ron Clark, sat down next to me. He listened to my harsh self-criticism and gently took my hand and said, "Jessika, what would you tell your best friend if she were in your situation?" In that powerful moment, I realized that, while we all have to struggle through Stage 2 over and over and over, the best way to get through it is to be kind, loving, and supportive of ourselves. We need an inner coach and best friend to help us. While we also need supportive teachers, coaches, and friends who remind us of our brilliance, we must learn how to do that for ourselves first and foremost.

SELF-REFLECTIVE EXERCISE:

1. Describe attributes of your inner coach. For example, he or she is supportive, loving, or challenging. Make a list of at least five attributes.

1. _____

2. _____

3. _____

4. _____

5. _____

2. Share what your inner coach wants for you. For example: "My inner coach wants me to blossom into a graceful and technical performer." Or, "My inner coach wants me to enjoy every moment I am on a dance floor."

_____

_____

_____

3. When you are being overly critical of yourself, what would your inner coach or your best friend say?

_____

_____

_____

4. What do you need to do to remind yourself of the support you have from your inner coach when things are difficult or challenging?

_____

_____

_____

_____

EXPERT ADVICE:

RON CLARK AND LINDA CARPENTER
ARE INSTRUCTORS AND CO-OWNERS OF DANCE PLUS BALLROOM IN COLUMBUS, OHIO.

JF: Ron, you have taught ballroom dancing for more than 40 years and have a fan page on Facebook with more than 1,000 people who have danced with you over the years. What is the most common self-criticism you hear from students?

RON: *Students often become frustrated at a certain point in their dancing and begin to doubt themselves. They'll say, "I can't do it," or "I'm not going to be able to learn how to do that," and the truth is that they all can. What stops them is their fear and negative self-talk. They create internal obstacles that are often rooted in other issues, such as self-doubt and unhappiness. The way I look at it, obstacles are only patterns that reappear in your life. How you handle them is what matters most.*

JF: Linda, as a female instructor working mostly with men and couples, what are some of the self-limiting beliefs you tend to hear?

LINDA: *It surprises me how many students aren't willing to hear positive feedback. Instead, they insist on focusing on what they don't do well even when they are actually doing the steps correctly. My rule for those students is that they are not allowed to say things like "I'm not doing that right," or "It doesn't feel right," when they, in fact, are. It's hard to convince people to be gentle and nice to themselves.*

JF: What advice would you share with dancers who tend to be overly hard on themselves while going through Stage 2?

RON: *Hug other students or your instructor to relieve the stress. Physical touch can be such a powerful tool, and it puts you in a different state of mind.*

LINDA: *Listen to your instructor when he or she gives you positive feedback. I remind my students that I am the professional and that they are in good hands. I tell them that if I say they are doing something well or correctly, I don't want to hear any negative back talk. Our lessons then become a place for encouraging growth and positive changes.*

ACTION STEP:

DANCING TIP 6 / Write down or memorize a supportive statement that your inner coach or best friend would say to help you through a tough time in your dancing. If you are a visual learner, find a picture or a magazine clipping of something that reminds you of the same message. I have a picture in my mind of Grace Kelly that my inner coach shares with me when things get tough. My goal is to be a graceful, classy, and generous dancer, and to me, her picture helps me to reconnect with my true center. I may not be the best dancer on the floor, but I can always be generous, loving, and supportive of those around me.

COACHING TIP 6 / Consider the other parts of your life where you could use an inner coach. In what situations might you be overly harsh on yourself that your inner coach could offer insight and advice? It may be that you love your work and spend long hours at the office, which brings you home to your family later than you would like. What would your inner coach tell you about your work/life balance? What would your inner coach tell your family about your love for your work? If you find it helpful, write down statements for each family member and share them with those you love. Ask for their feedback or input. Sometimes, opening up the dialogue is all you need to do to gain additional support from those around you.

"I WILL...."

STEP 4 / IDENTIFY AND MAXIMIZE YOUR STRENGTHS, THEN WORK ON YOUR WEAKNESSES

"IF I HAD SIX HOURS TO CHOP DOWN A TREE. I'D SPEND THE FIRST FOUR HOURS **SHARPENING THE AXE.**"

—ABRAHAM LINCOLN

Most of my clients hire me because they want to eliminate a negative behavior or fix something that isn't working for them. The first thing I do is to help them identify and maximize their strengths. Isn't that contradictory?

Research clearly shows that when we tap in to our strong points and focus our work and attention on them, we significantly increase our effectiveness and results. **If we over-focus on our weaknesses, our productivity, motivation, and performance go down the drain.**

What never ceases to amaze me is how uncomfortable my clients are when I ask them to name or verbally share their positive qualities. They often begin by saying something like, "I'm pretty good at..." or "I think I'm okay at...." Mind you, these are executives running multimillion-dollar organizations and leading teams of hundreds of people, but they are uncomfortable owning their strengths!

Why is it that most of us are so shy about discussing our virtues? While the answer may differ from person to person, I believe that most people are taught early on not to brag about ourselves. Instead, we begin to hide our self-praise by using tentative such words as "sort of" or "I think," so other people don't see us as bragging. While being humble is certainly a wonderful trait, being unclear or dismissive of our talents is not. It actually causes our brains and bodies much confusion and can really mess with our thinking.

As dancers, we have to consider two types of strengths—physical and mental/emotional. The first group is often easier to identify. For example, I have always known that my strongest physical asset was my legs. Even as a child, I had powerful quad muscles and was attracted to running, basketball, and soccer. When I started ballroom dancing, I quickly realized that maximizing my leg strength would be important. It also comes easiest to me, so it's an all-around win-win. That is how our strengths work: We can put a lot less effort into developing and using them, and they bring us the most rewards.

The mental/emotional strengths tend to be a bit more complicated, and most people are not as clear about what they are or how to embrace them. Instead, we have learned to minimize these characteristics, which causes our brains and bodies unnecessary confusion. Let's say, for example, that you know without much doubt that you are a compassionate person, yet you dismiss positive feedback or compliments around this trait, which creates a message to your brain that being compassionate is not such a big deal. Trust me, it is. There are plenty of people out there who can't show compassion!

Simply thank people for compliments, and embrace your gifts and build on them. My good friend and fellow dancer, Kristen Wheeler, has coined the term **"strength afterglow,"** which I love. It's the feeling we get when we are working and interacting from this approach. We walk around "in the zone" or with a heavenly smile on our faces when we feel great about who we are and what we have to offer the world.

There is, however, an inherent danger in over-focusing on a strength. **Any strength overextended can become a weakness.** To be a great dancer, you need to be balanced. The key is to work on improving areas that hold you back and maximize what you are really great at. This strategy helps to build confidence and competence.

SELF-REFLECTIVE EXERCISE:

1. Make a list of at least three physical strengths you have as a dancer. Don't worry about putting them in the right order. Simply list them. When done, identify at least one strategy for each that will help maximize your dancing practice or performance. For example, maybe you have strong feet. A maximizing strategy could be to highlight your feet in an upcoming show dance or routine.

PHYSICAL STRENGTH	MAXIMIZING STRATEGY
1.	1.
2.	2.
3.	3.
4.	4.

2. Repeat the above exercise with at least three mental/emotional strengths you have as a dancer. For example, you could list that you are open to feedback with a strategy to attend a workshop/dance camp or hire a coach to offer you additional insight.

MENTAL/EMOTIONAL STRENGTH	MAXIMIZING STRATEGY
1.	1.
2.	2.
3.	3.
4.	4.

Great work! Now, let's spend a little time reviewing weaknesses. Notice that I say "a little time." Over focusing on weak points is dangerous, as it can erode confidence and enjoyment. I know some coaches who are so intensely focused on improving dancers' shortcomings that the dancers slowly but surely begins to beat up on themselves, and their dancing skills actually decrease. Kristen Wheeler calls it a **"weakness hangover."** Too much focusing on our weaknesses causes us to feel sluggish and tired. We show up to the world with just half of who we are, and we can become really angry about it.

The key is to identify our imperfections and work on them in conjunction with our assets. As with strengths, we have physical and mental/emotional weaknesses. The physical ones are easy; the mental/emotional ones are a different story.

We all have physical limitations. It may be that we are hitting a certain age where our stamina is diminishing or our bones ache. Or it may be that we have limited range of motion due to injuries or surgeries. Once we have identified and embraced our physical challenges, we need to create strategies for overcoming them. Some shortcomings we can change and some we can't. But we can always change our attitudes.

I have a screw and a wire from a bunionectomy in the big toe of my right foot, which limits range of motion in the foot. When I mentioned this to my coach—who is not amused by any excuses—he asked, "What are you doing to compensate for it?" Honestly, I had never even considered it. I just took it as a fact and kept restating it as if it were a perfectly acceptable reason for not performing at my best. Great dancers move beyond their deficiencies and minimize the focus on them.

SELF-REFLECTIVE EXERCISE:

3. List three of your most challenging physical weaknesses as a dancer and strategies to minimize them. For example, one might be that you easily get out of breath and can dance for only 10 minutes without taking a break. An action plan to overcome this may be to work with a personal trainer once a week or to join a local gym for cardio and weight training.

PHYSICAL WEAKNESS	MINIMIZING STRATEGY
1.	1.
2.	2.
3.	3.
4.	4.

4. List at least three mental/emotional weaknesses that stand in the way of your being the dancer you desire. It may be that you are sensitive to criticism from your instructor or coach and you make excuses for a lack of performance. A minimizing strategy might be to simply accept the feedback and thank the instructor or coach without judgment.

MENTAL/EMOTIONAL WEAKNESS	MINIMIZING STRATEGY
1.	1.
2.	2.
3.	3.
4.	4.

EXPERT ADVICE:

KRISTEN WHEELER IS A BUSINESS COACH, A CONTEMPORARY DANCER AND A DANCE/MOVEMENT THERAPIST IN BOULDER, COLORADO.

JF: Kristen, you are a business coach who focuses on working with clients from a perspective of strengths. You are also a dancer and a dance/movement therapist. What would you say is the most important thing to know about identifying and maximizing strengths as a dancer?

KRISTEN: *It's really simple. Follow what feels natural and good. That is how you'll find your strengths. Too often, we don't trust our own instincts and bodies. If we do what feels good, we are usually in a place of love. Love is a mega-motivator. Unfortunately, we often get disconnected from our love of an activity that drew us to it in the first place. It is a crushing tyranny to focus entirely on doing well vs. feeling the love. And what is dance anyway, except radiating love or something like it?*

Be specific about what your favorite part of dancing is—not what parts of dancing you're good at, but what parts make you light up. It might be invisible to you, so consider asking a trusted observer of your dancing. Then give that your attention and investment. You'll have an appetite to practice and get even better at what makes you light up. Contrary to conventional wisdom, that's where you'll grow the most, not in your areas of weakness.

JF: Is there a formula or a percentage of time that you recommend for someone to spend identifying or working on their weaknesses?

KRISTEN: *Ideally, you are spending most of your time investing in your strengths. Everyone will find his way to that balance differently. Focus on your weaknesses only enough that they don't derail you. In other words, know what your imperfections are and be functional with them. We are all taught to focus on shortcomings, so it's automatic. But it's kryptonite for your confidence, so be careful. You may find that you need to tip your investment in your strengths one tiny step at a time, because it will probably feel strange at first. You may need to make a "weakness sandwich" by practicing a strong point before and after a weak one so that you don't wear yourself out.*

ACTION STEP:

DANCING TIP 7 / Commit to developing at least one dancing strength (physical or mental/emotional) this month. Start by identifying a specific quality, then set a goal for enhancing it and describe what that would look like. Next, identify what you think is needed to take you there and create measurable action steps with defined timelines. For example, "One of my dancing strengths is my leg action. My goal is to show a clear American Style action by moving from using a bent to a soft knee in my rumba. I commit to doing flexed walk rumba walks for 10 minutes three days per week for a month. At the end of this exercise, my goal is to naturally deliver a soft knee."

It may be especially helpful to connect with your instructor and determine the parameters and milestones for this exercise together. That way, you are sure that it is consistent with your development plan and that your instructor can help hold you accountable and give you feedback. Remember, the dancing community is very supportive, and it isn't unusual for random people who have never met you to come up and offer compliments and feedback on your dancing. Get in the habit of offering positive feedback to others also. The more you spread it around, the more comfortable you will be accepting it yourself.

COACHING TIP 7 / Get used to receiving positive feedback, on and off the dance floor. Gracefully accept it by simply saying, "thank you" or "I appreciate the feedback." There is such a great joy in giving and receiving feedback. Make it a daily practice to offer at least one positive statement, thought or action to a person you meet. It can be a friend, family member, or complete stranger. Notice how you feel when you offer someone else a compliment. As you get more comfortable giving feedback, notice how you respond when it is given to you. Are you able to embrace it? Are you resisting it? What does it feel like when you embrace it and thank the other person for offering their opinion and thoughts? My good friend, Barbara Wayman, keeps a receiving journal in which she records any gifts, comments, or nice acts on a daily basis. It helps her be grateful and allows her to focus on the positive things that come her way.

"I WILL...."

STEP 5 / WHEN AT STAGE 2, DON'T OVER RELY ON YOUR FEELINGS; SEEK OUT AND TRUST THE ADVICE OF EXPERTS

"DO NOT GIVE TOO MUCH TO FEELINGS. AN OVERLY SENSITIVE HEART IS AN UNHAPPY POSSESSION ON THIS SHAKY EARTH."

— JOHANN WOLFGANG VON GOETHE

Going through Stage 2 is emotional; there is just no way around it. The key to successfully moving through this stage is to remember that feelings come and go. Just because we feel something, it doesn't mean that is an accurate reflection of our circumstances. If we over rely on our feelings as we go through Stage 2, we often end up limiting our dancing progress and our chances of reaching the next level.

We are going to feel what we are going to feel. There is nothing we can do about it. **Trying to control feelings is like trying to restrain a tidal wave.** The more we resist, the more a feeling persists. Picture yourself trying to hold back tears after hearing devastating news. Or, imagine not being upset when someone you care about makes an intentionally hurtful comment about you. You may argue, "I don't show it if I get hurt." That may be true, but no matter how well you are able to control your emotions, you feel them nevertheless.

It is easy to think that what we feel represents reality. Most of the time, it does not. Instead, an emotional trigger may be rooted in previous experiences, old pain, or dysfunctional patterns. This is especially true during Stage 2, when our emotions tend to be self-critical or based in our insecurities. This is not the time to depend on them and interpret them as fact. It is extremely important to consider what a feeling actually means, where it comes from, and how helpful or hurtful it may be.

A friend of mine, we will call her Liz, was frustrated that she wasn't progressing fast enough in her dancing. She was upset with her instructor and coaches for not pushing her at the pace she expected. She was afraid of not meeting her aggressive dancing goals and began to feel unsure and angry. Were her feelings valid? Yes. Were they an indication of her perceived reality? Yes, but that doesn't make them a *true* reflection of her circumstances. Let me explain in a bit more detail.

Looking at Liz's situation objectively, we learn that Liz, who is a very talented dancer, desires to be a top amateur competitor in a few years. She is a fast learner and has a tendency to get bored with repetitive exercises. She loves to learn new steps and challenge herself by increasing the level of difficulty in her moves. These are wonderful traits, and they helped her progress quickly through the first stages of her dancing. Lately, however, her instructor and coaches have encouraged her to slow down and work on perfecting her basic movements. Remember, Liz doesn't like repetitive exercises and these requests make her feel that she is being held back. In most sports, an athlete reaches a point where he or she has to slow down and even go back to basics to propel forward faster and with greater skill. So Liz's instructor and coaches, who have years of experience, are telling her to slow down and work more on her basics. Chances are that they are right. Yet Liz *feels* with every bone in her body that they are wrong, and she trusts her feelings. Who is right? The odds are that the instructor and coaches are. The mistake Liz is making is over relying on her feelings during a time when she is in emotional turmoil.

There are, of course, other times when trusting our gut feelings help us to make important and valuable decisions. They tend to be made with successful outcomes when we are at stages 3 and 4, but not as much at stages 1 or 2.

Dan Millman writes in his book *Body Mind Mastery: Creating Success in Sport and Life* about the importance of listening to others during Stage 2 of athletic development:

> As a high school freshman, Tom Weeden decided that he wanted to become one of the nation's premier gymnasts—not an unusual goal for many young athletes. What was unusual was that Tom methodically sought advice from every coach he could find. As one

of those coaches, I suggested that he begin by developing strength, suppleness, and correct fundamentals before he concentrated on fancy skills—advice I had shared with any young athlete. But Tom had the patience and wisdom to actually follow this advice. While other gymnasts were making a name for themselves, Tom worked quietly and diligently on his talent foundation. Then, about a year later, he suddenly began winning every competition he entered. First he won local events, then regional, then national—until Tom Weeden made the United States Olympic Team.

While we are at Stage 2, it is imperative that we acknowledge our feelings, talk to our instructors and coaches about them, and recognize that we may not be the best judges of our dancing progress at this time. As you transition into stages 3 and 4, you may find that your confidence increases, and that is a great time to trust your feelings and emotions again.

SELF-REFLECTIVE EXERCISE:

1. List at least five negative or destructive emotions that you are experiencing about your dancing, such as impatience, frustration, nervousness, or stress.

_____

_____

_____

2. What do you need from your instructor, coaches, and other supportive individuals to check in on the accuracy of these feelings? What questions may you need to ask them to help you move past these feelings into reality?

_____

_____

_____

3. What do you need to ask yourself about these feelings? For example, you may need to check in on why you are feeling impatient or stressed. Is it because you are afraid you won't be able to take your dancing to the next level? Or do you have a tendency to blame others instead of looking to see what you may be contributing to the feeling or situation you are in? Being honest with yourself and your instructor will enable you to propel forward much faster.

_____

_____

_____

4. What can you do to move past these emotions and feelings (even though they may feel real to you) and take a more objective look at your dancing?

_____

_____

_____

EXPERT ADVICE:

PIERRE ALLAIRE AND MIREILLE VEILLEUX HOLD THE IMPRESSIVE TITLES OF CANADIAN PROFESSIONAL 10 DANCE CHAMPIONS AND CANADIAN AND NORTH AMERICAN PROFESSIONAL MODERN CHAMPIONS, AND THEY WERE BRITISH RISING STAR LATIN CHAMPIONS AT BLACKPOOL. THEY ARE PREMIER ADJUDICATORS AND COACHES AT BALLROOM STUDIOS AROUND THE WORLD. THEY RESIDE IN MONTREAL, QUEBEC, CANADA.

JF: You have seen your fair share of emotional dancers and competitors. What would you say is the biggest mistake that dancers make when they rely on their feelings while in the middle of Stage 2?

PIERRE: *Dancing is an emotional sport, and experienced dancers have learned how to tap in to their feelings to excel at their craft. New or inexperienced dancers who are in the middle of Stage 2 for the first time don't yet have the knowledge or insight that comes with going through Stage 2 over and over again or how to manage emotions to their benefit. They have to remember that they are growing and developing at this stage and the emotions that come with this experience are natural. They must be patient with themselves and not let feelings hold them back. This is where having a great coach makes a difference. A seasoned coach knows how to help students connect their physical and emotional beings and move them through the process with greater ease and confidence. As a coach, I always care about what my students feel and look like. Once students move through stages 3 and 4, they develop greater emotional intelligence. I remind them to use their brains when they practice and their hearts when they dance or perform.*

MIREILLE: *When you are at Stage 2, it is easy to make decisions too quickly. A student needs to take the time to think about a situation that has become emotional and talk it through with the coach or instructor. It's important to have a coach and/or instructor you can rely on to guide you in the right direction when emotions are confusing or distracting. Stage 2 is something all dancers, no matter how experienced, go through. This means that all coaches and instructors have gone through similar emotions and have been successful in moving past them to reach their dancing goals. Tapping in to their years of experience is the key. This is why it is important that students take the time to find the right coach or instructor.*

JF: *What tips would you give to dancers who are in the middle of Stage 2 and are experiencing feelings and emotions about their lack of progress or results?*

PIERRE: *Repetition is the key to becoming a great dancer. Dance, dance, dance, and then dance some more. One of my favorite techniques is to use technology. I encourage students to view videos of others and try to emulate the techniques and feelings they see in the experienced dancers on the tapes. It is also extremely helpful to get recordings of your own dancing so you can truly see yourself the way others do. I also advice students to make good use of mirrors. Pick a movement or step and exaggerate the motion. Do you look in the mirror the way you picture yourself in your mind? Is the reflection in the mirror how you want to look? If not, what changes do you need to make to reach the next level? Record the sensations you feel as you watch yourself in the mirror. The key is to increase your self-awareness and come up with strategies for developing your dancing.*

MIREILLE: *You need to be able to talk to your coach and trust that he or she has your best interests at heart. When you observe prospective coaches, look at both their dancing accomplishments and how they live their lives. Is how they approach life, other students, and the ballroom community a reflection of your own values? Does the coach produce the type of students you can relate to or wish to emulate? If you have the right coach, you will be able to take his or her advice during times when emotions can otherwise get in the way. A great coach will help students understand that sometimes the quickest way to move forward is to go back to basics. Dancing is always about working on the fundamentals. Sometimes, the higher we get in our dancing, the easier it is to forget about the basics. If you are getting frustrated or emotional because you can't push through to the next level, go back and work on the basics you already know. This will build confidence and skills that you will need as you move forward.*

ACTION STEP:

DANCING TIP 8 / In your dancing notebook, draw four columns down a page. In the first column, list five of the most commonly challenging emotions or feelings you have regarding your dancing. In the second column, write when each feeling tends to occur. For example, a challenging feeling could be insecurity, which shows up when others are watching you dance, such as during a show dance when you are the only couple on the floor. In the third column, list the frequency of occurrence. You may use a numbers system, such as a 1-5 scale (1 = infrequently and 5 = frequently). In the fourth column, indicate if you tend to blame others or yourself when that feeling occurs. For example, if you feel insecure when others watch you, do you take your insecurities out on your instructor (externally) or do you beat yourself up with negative self-talk (internally)? Review your list and look for a pattern. In the final column, list an action step you will take the next time that feeling occurs. It can be that you will stop the negative self-talk or that you will apologize to your instructor for taking your feelings out on him or her. This exercise is meant to increase your self-awareness around your feelings and learn how to handle them.

COACHING TIP 8 / Living too much in our feelings can get us in a lot of trouble. In what other parts of your life may you be over relying on feelings and emotions when a more objective approach would serve you better? Make a list of at least one other area and write a short paragraph describing the situation. For example, you may realize that when you deal with a certain family member you tend to be overly judgmental or focused on that person's need to change instead of looking at what you can or should change about yourself to get a different outcome. Or it may be that at work, you react emotionally and don't get the results you want.

Once you have identified a specific situation, design an action statement for how to neutralize your feelings and move into a more objective, non-emotional approach. For example, if you have a tendency to move in to judging others when you feel emotional, an action step might be: "The next time I interact with Susan and notice that I am judging her or telling her what to do, I will refrain from giving advice and just listen. Afterward, I will do a fair-minded audit of myself and write one or more things I can do to move my life in a more positive direction instead of focusing my energies on trying to fix her."

"I WILL...."

CHAPTER THREE

STEP 6 / EMBRACE YOUR OWN DANCING JOURNEY AND STAY ON THE PATH

"TO REALIZE ONE'S DESTINY IS A PERSON'S ONLY OBLIGATION…AND WHEN YOU WANT SOMETHING, ALL **THE UNIVERSE CONSPIRES IN HELPING YOU TO ACHIEVE IT.**"

— PAULO COELHO

As you work your way through Stage 2, you will find that things become clearer and easier. If you have embraced and used the exercises in the previous five steps in this chapter, you will have developed increased self-awareness, confidence in your dancing, and a sense of accomplishment. **You know from reading the experts' advice that you are not alone on this journey.** All dancers have gone through the pains and challenges you are experiencing at Stage 2. With a lot of the "head trash" gone, it's time to embrace your own dancing journey!

The last challenge at Stage 2 concerns the tendency we may have to compare ourselves to other dancers and wonder why our paths and progress differs from theirs. We may look at dancers who had similar starting points to ours and become either judgmental of them or overly harsh with ourselves for not reaching the same milestones and accomplishments. If you have begun to compete, it is natural but dangerous to compare yourself with others. The fact is that, when you compete, judges compare you to other dancers and that is how they make decisions about who places where or who gets called back in each heat. **Leave the judging and evaluating to the professionals!**

Early in my competing experience, I focused on how long others had danced to find comparisons or a system for assessing my own skill level. What I have learned as an intermediate competitor is that this is utterly useless.

One of my close friends was feeling down about her dancing progress and told me, "Jessika, I'm so bummed because you've danced for a year-and-a-half and I've danced for a year, but you're so much more advanced than I am." I replied, "Jane, the first year I danced I took five lessons a week. You took one a week. That's probably why I advanced faster." It is not helpful to compare your dancing to that of others because you may be missing out on the details of their dance journeys.

They may take ten times the amount of lessons you do or they may have come to ballroom dancing with ten years of previous dance experience. They may learn faster than you do or they may have different financial resources. For the sake of your sanity and your dancing enjoyment, stop—or, even better, never start—comparing yourself to others. Instead, go back to the exercises we did in Chapter 2 and reconnect with your dance passion. Remember why you dance in the first place and recall your dancing goals.

One of my strategies to ensure that I stay grounded on my own dancing path is to set a goal for each competition or milestone. After an event or heat, I check in with my goals to see if I am staying on track. It may sound simple, but it some times isn't. It takes practice.

For example, at the 2010 Ohio Star Ball, my goal was to perform a show dance in the Best of the Best challenge without making any visible mistakes. This was especially important to me as my very first show dance, a few months prior, had ended in disaster because I blanked out and forgot my entire routine. My instructor and I had had only two months to design and rehearse the Best of the Best routine, so my goal wasn't to win the entire challenge. I wanted just to dance well, be proud of my performance, and enjoy the experience. Of course, I really wanted to place in the top six, but I have learned not to make placement a goal. There are too many variables that go in to that decision over which I have no control.

After we performed, I felt fantastic! We didn't make any major errors, and I remembered my complete routine. My instructor and I celebrated by sharing positive thoughts and feedback. But when we learned that we placed seventh, I was suddenly so disappointed. I began beating up on myself for letting down my instructor.

We found a quiet area to talk, and I began to say out loud all the things that I was feeling. My instructor stopped me and asked, "Didn't you meet all the goals that you had set? Then why are you so upset? I'm proud of you. I'm really happy with our dancing and I believe in you. What we did today is completely in alignment with your dance goals." It took me a few minutes to realize that he was absolutely right. I had fallen into the trap of comparing myself to other dancers.

The truth was that the judges who watched us liked something better in the other competitors, for a million reasons that I couldn't even begin to guess. If I tried to figure out why, I would be focusing on others' dance journeys and not my own. I'm not saying you shouldn't audit yourself and your dancing. That can be a great exercise to improve your skills. What isn't helpful is when you compare your dance experience to someone else's, which you have little to no information about.

I find that when I keep my attention on my own path and dancing goals, I'm happier, more at peace, and I enjoy my sport so much more. I dance because I love it, and I believe that I live my true purpose when I dance. So why do I compare myself to others? Why do I spend time and energy wanting to be somewhere else when where I am is absolutely perfect? My answers to these questions are usually the same: because I have lost focus on my passion, and I have become unbalanced in my dancing.

If this resonates with you and you sense that you may be falling into the comparison trap, work through the next set of self-reflective exercises. I have found that when I re-center and re-ground myself, my dancing frequently improves and develops effortlessly. Dan Millman summarizes this step perfectly in his book *Body Mind Mastery*:

> *Masters of one art have mastered all because they have mastered themselves. With dominion over both mind and muscle, they demonstrate power, serenity, and spirit. They not only have talent for sport, they have an expanded capacity for life. The experts shine in the competitive arena: masters shine everywhere.*

SELF-REFLECTIVE EXERCISE:

1. Write the reasons you dance. For example, it may make you feel good or provides an outlet for stress, or just because you love it. Begin the sentence "I dance because..."

_____

_____

_____

2. Write two of your most important dancing goals or milestones.

_____

_____

_____

3. List one strategy for staying on your path and reminding yourself about your own dance journey.

_____

_____

_____

4. List your most powerful or seductive derailer or trap. What situation, scenario, or person may make you question your own progress or process and get you off your dance path?

_____

_____

_____

5. How will you ensure that these derailers don't affect your dance experience?

_____

_____

_____

EXPERT ADVICE:

BRENDAN AND CHRISTINA DONELSON
ARE HUSBAND AND WIFE WHO COMPETE IN DIFFERENT LEVELS IN PRO/AM EVENTS. THEY LIVE IN NASHVILLE, TENN.

JF: Brendan and Christina, you both compete as ballroom dancers, but at different levels and do not compete together. Instead, you both dance with top instructors who carry a lot of different students. How do you avoid comparing yourself to other students or to each other?

BRENDAN: *I don't really compare myself to my instructor Shalene's other dancers because I trust that she puts me where she thinks I would have the best chance of winning. There are times that I might notice her students, and even times where I watch their lessons and learn, but I don't really feel much in the way of comparing myself. My wife says I will care more when I get better.*

As far as comparing myself with Christina, I don't think I'm in her league. Her rhythm is awesome and she's a performer. I feel like I am still just learning the basics and getting to a performance level where I can eventually loosen up and dance. I have excelled at Smooth, and we enjoy the lessons with Shalene we sometimes take together. It's a huge help to me when I get to dance with Christina and see where Shalene may be somewhat "back leading" me instead of me leading her. I encourage any amateur men to dance with other amateur women to see what they are not doing/leading.

CHRISTINA: *This is easy. We don't even consider comparing ourselves to others or to each other. It is an independent sport, not a team sport. I just do the best I can. Brendan and I believe completely in what our instructors and coaches tell us, and because we do that, our results show that we are on the right path."*

JF: What tips would you give to amateur students to help them stay on their own dancing journey or path?

BRENDAN: *As far as staying on path, here's my motto: I do this because my wife enjoys it so much, and I have such an amazing teacher. It's like exercise and competition blended into one, plus it's mentally stimulating. Because of all those factors, I will continue. And, I'm having fun. If any of those things change, I might reconsider, but otherwise it's a great sport for my wife and me to compete in for a long time.*

CHRISTINA: *When you first start to dance or compete, it is easy to get caught up in comparing yourself with others. Instead of observing those in your skill level or age category, observe the dancers in more advanced categories. This will inspire you rather than discourage you. When I began to compete, I watched the final rounds of those who made it and those who were doing open work and tried to emulate what they were doing. It truly helped me take my dancing to the next level. If you want to advance your dancing, strive to be the best version of you that you can be.*

ACTION STEP:

DANCING TIP 9 / Set a goal for each competition or milestone in your dancing. Avoid making it about placements or anything that involves other people's opinions or evaluations. Make sure that the goal is connected to the core reason you dance. Share it with your instructor and ask him or her to remind you to stay on track. Reward yourself when you meet your goal or milestone and celebrate with your instructor. After all, if you wanted to do a solo sport, you may have chosen gymnastics or ballet. You dance with a partner for a reason. Remember to include him or her in your successes.

COACHING TIP 9 / Consider the other parts of your life where you may compare yourself to others. Reflect on your interactions with coworkers, family, or friends. Consider how you feel when you do. Do you beat yourself up? Do you feel superior? What does comparing yourself to others do for you? After reflecting on your feelings, write an action statement that you will take to stop the comparisons. For example, it may be that you compare your financial situation or your parenting skills to those of your friends. An action step may be to remind yourself that you don't have all the facts about that person's situation and that your journey is different than theirs. Another one is to make a list of all the things in your life that you are grateful for. Make it a goal to never compare yourself to someone else, but if you fall off the wagon, gently forgive yourself and get back on track. I promise you that nothing good will come from focusing your time and energy on others at the expense of your own journey.

"I WILL...."

CHAPTER 4:

EMBRACING STAGE 3

"DON'T WISH IT WERE EASIER, WISH YOU WERE BETTER."

— JIM ROHN

Once we have emerged at the other end of Stage 2, things begin to look up again. **Self-confidence and increased motivation have replaced feelings of inadequacy and self-doubt.** You tend to feel a sense of renewal and determination to reach your next set of dancing goals. These are the rewards for pushing yourself through Stage 2. You begin to feel a sense of accomplishment.

At Stage 3, we know what we know, and we can begin to polish our dancing techniques and reach breakthroughs that we struggled to comprehend at Stage 2. That doesn't mean that our learning and development stops at Stage 3. Instead, this is where we begin to do a lot more self-reflection and internal processing. We are able to catch ourselves and autocorrect movements before our instructors or coaches do. We know what we need to do and we can identify what we need to work on.

I remember watching other competitors at one of the largest U.S. Pro/Am competitions after about nine months of dancing. For the first time, I could identify the nuances between dancers with correct postures, good technique, and exceptional showmanship. Earlier, at stages 1 and 2, I thought that if it looked good to me, they were doing it correctly.

At Stage 3, I also began reviewing video recordings of my own dancing, and I could easily identify what I needed to work on. I bought several DVDs and watched YouTube videos of professional dancers teaching techniques, which I began practicing on my own to reinvigorate my progress.

STEP 1 / CHALLENGE YOURSELF AND PRACTICE YOUR CRAFT DAILY

"BY THREE METHODS WE MAY **LEARN WISDOM**: FIRST, **BY REFLECTION**, WHICH IS NOBLEST; SECOND, **BY IMITATION**, WHICH IS EASIEST; AND THIRD **BY EXPERIENCE**, WHICH IS BITTEREST."

— CONFUCIUS

When I began dancing, I was fortunate enough to be able to take four or five lessons per week. This strategy allowed me to advance my dancing faster, and I moved through the stages at a quick pace. In addition to private lessons, I also immersed myself in reading anything and everything I could on dancing techniques, including syllabuses, books, and autobiographies of dancers to learn what I needed to do to polish my techniques. I committed to practicing one hour per day and took copious notes after each lesson to give myself "homework." I also hired coaches to work with both me and my instructor to get an external perspective and to receive advice about the competitive ballroom landscape.

For some of you, this may seem a bit much, and it may not be consistent with your own dancing goals. My initial dancing goal was to see how good I could get, and my "Type A" personality pushed me to move more aggressively than most students.

I was amazed to learn that **most professional dancers do exactly what we amateurs have to do**. They practice the same move over and over again and spend most of their time working on their basics. They practice every day and find a system or a process that they repeat to hone their skills daily.

For the next self-reflective exercise, pick the ones that are consistent with your own dancing goals. There are no right or wrong ways to practice your craft!

SELF-REFLECTIVE EXERCISE:

1. Circle the strategy that you believe will most help you as you progress through Stage 3 or assist your dancing at this stage. Select one that you don't currently use or don't use as effectively as you know you could:

→ Practice by yourself for 30 minutes to one hour three times per week.

→ Take notes after your lessons and assign yourself at least one piece of homework to practice before your next lesson.

→ Buy, rent, or borrow a dance technique DVD and pick one part to practice by yourself. It is always recommended that you check with your instructor before getting a DVD to ensure that the techniques are up-to-date and accurate. Dancing techniques change often.

→ Borrow or buy dancing books to learn more about how to best partner with your instructor and what it takes to keep your attitude and skills at peak capacity. For recommended readings, please see the resource section at the back of this book.

→ Buy or borrow a copy of your studio's syllabus and pick one dance and one step to practice. Memorize the steps, footwork, alignments, amount of sway, and other details of the steps. Pick one dance and one step and ask your instructor to quiz you on your knowledge during your next lesson.

→ Ask your instructor or coach to summarize a specific part of your dancing that you need to improve. Use a camera or phone to record him or her doing it. Set aside 30 minutes of practice time to repeat the lesson over and over to improve your dancing.

→ Spend time budgeting the money you have for dancing. Consider where it can best be spent. Is it on additional lessons, coaching sessions, costumes, or parties? Remember to allocate your resources so they take you closer to your dancing goals.

→ Practice your steps and routines in your head. It is an excellent exercise because it forces you to think through each step, movement, and motion. When you do, you have to picture yourself doing it perfectly. This mental exercise sharpens your mental dancing acumen.

EXPERT ADVICE:

DECHO KRAEV AND BREE WATSON
ARE WORLD RHYTHM CHAMPIONS AND NATIONAL RHYTHM FINALIST RUNNERS UP. THEY ARE INSTRUCTORS AND COACHES IN PHOENIX, ARIZ.

JF: You are the World Rhythm Champions and have danced professionally for almost 10 years. What do you do on a daily or weekly basis to ensure that you challenge yourself and polish your craft?

DACHO: *We have a routine that we follow almost every day. First, we have coffee. I'm a Starbucks nut! Then we warm up. Because of Bree's advanced movements, she has to warm up longer than I do. Once we are warmed up, we practice our basic figures by ourselves for about 10 to 15 minutes. Once we are in the right dancing frame of mind, we do our basic figures together for another 10 to 15 minutes. During this time, we connect with each other to make sure that we are aligned. It is a great time to check in on our routines and to verify that we are both in agreement with any changes or adjustments we may have decided to incorporate since the last time we practiced. After that, we do one or two rounds of our competitive routines to awaken our muscle memory. Finally, we take a look at the parts of our routines that may be bothering us or that we want to correct. Dancing is constant practice and repetition."*

BREE: *There is no "magic pill." It's practice, practice, practice and then some more practice. I always smile when my students ask me how long it will take them to get a certain move or to take their dancing to the next level. The truth is that I don't know. It depends on how much they are willing to practice, how far their natural talents will take them, and their commitment to their dancing. I advise my students to come in early and warm up, practice their routines, and stay after if they can to get the most out of their lessons.*

I'm a bit of a perfectionist, and my internal drive propels me to always work a little harder and to push a bit more. Dancing is hard work and requires determination. If you do something a little bit more or work a little harder each time you practice, your efforts will add up.

JF: What two tips would you share with dancers who want to polish their dancing or break through to the next level?

DECHO: *I'll keep it short. You have to love what you do and do what you love.*

BREE: *Stay focused on your dancing goals. It's so easy to get down on yourself and lose momentum. The truth is that we all have those feelings, but you have to stay focused and not give up. When I sense these feelings in myself, I recall a moment when things seemed to just flow in my dancing, and I remember why I love dancing so much. This helps me to press past the challenging emotions that come with any physical and mental sport. Remember that going beyond just "good" or "good enough" will bring great rewards. You may find that by pushing yourself beyond what you currently think you can do enables you to grow both as a dancer and a person. If you truly want to take your dancing to the next level, you have to enjoy the process of learning. Results will come if you are open to new information, opinions, and feedback.*

ACTION STEP:

DANCING TIP 10 / Select one action step or activity that you commit to working on for the next month. Set aside at least 30 minutes a day to practice it. Share your tip with your instructor to ensure that you are aligned with what he or she has planned for you.

COACHING TIP 10 / Commit to an activity or action step for a specific amount of time and duration that will help your overall health or well-being. It may be to meditate for 15 minutes each day for a month or to drink at least four large glasses of water each day. You may commit to taking your vitamins daily for a month or to do a random act of kindness every day for a week. The idea behind this tip is to identify a practice that brings you a physical, spiritual, or emotional benefit and then execute it consistently. After your designated time period, reflect on the changes in your mood or thought patterns. What are you noticing? How will it help you stay on track and commit to a practice? If you do maintain this focus, what benefits will you experience?

"I WILL...."

STEP 2 / ENTER A COMPETITION OR HIRE A COACH TO GET HONEST AND DIRECT FEEDBACK

"I BELIEVE IN GETTING INTO HOT WATER; IT KEEPS YOU CLEAN."

— G. K. CHESTERTON

One of my favorite aspects of dancing is competing. I love the thrill of going out on the floor and showing off the hard work my partner and I have put in. I value the feedback we get from judges who have seen us grow from competition to competition. I'm always humbled when they remember us and offer specific comments about how we have grown and where we still need to develop. If you are not competing and don't have access to this type of impartial feedback, **hire a dance coach or expert to evaluate your dancing.** At Stage 3 we have gone through a few painful rounds of Stage 2 and are usually ready to learn how to improve and polish our skills.

Although getting direct feedback isn't always fun, it will work wonders on moving you from where you are to where you want to be. I will never forget when premier professional coach, organizer of the Ohio Star Ball, and self-proclaimed "godfather of ballroom dancing" Sam Sodano told us after a heat, "You look dead out there!" He said it, as only Sam Sodano could, with brutal honesty but a supportive sparkle in his eye. His frank assessment definitely helped us to dial up our showmanship for the next heat and let go of our technical focus so we could enjoy the dancing.

Similarly, Linda Dean, a judge I respect tremendously, came up to me after a comp and said, "Your feet and legs are great, but what the heck are you doing with your upper body?" My honest answer was, "I don't know. What am I doing or, in this case, not doing?" She offered me some pointers, and as soon as I returned home I started working with my instructor and coach on my upper body. I recognized that I had focused so much on my feet and lower body movements that I hadn't even considered that my upper body was attached to it!

SELF-REFLECTIVE EXERCISE:

1. Think of a person in the world of ballroom dancing whom you admire. It can be an instructor, coach, organizer, or advanced dancer. Write out two questions about your dancing that you would like feedback on. For example, "If I could improve or focus on one thing in my dancing right now, what would it be?" Or, "What change can I make physically to improve the look of my dancing?"

Person I admire:

Question 1:

Question 2:

EXPERT ADVICE:

SAM SODANO IS THE ORGANIZER OF THE OHIO STAR BALL. HE IS A PREMIER ADJUDICATOR AND IS KNOW AS THE "GODFATHER OF BALLROOM DANCING." HE LIVES IN COLUMBUS, OHIO.

JF: What has been your motivation or inspiration to reach the impressive accomplishments you have in your life and career?

SAM: *I knew at a very early age what I wanted to do. I didn't have any external motivators or mentors. Instead, I relied on myself and focused intensely on what I wanted to accomplish. My internal drive and motivation has always been stronger than any external influences. I was just determined and committed, and I went for what I wanted. My true love for what I do is the source of my success.*

JF: What two tips would you give dancers who are close to breaking through to the next level of dancing but seem stuck?

SAM: *You have to love to dance. When you are truly committed to something, you work hard at it and your desire to break through to the next level is simply part of the process. Trust in your own abilities to accomplish what you want. Don't listen to naysayers who don't believe in your goals. Align yourself with people who are supportive and positive. You have to truly believe that you can accomplish your goals, even when they seem out of reach. Never stop believing in your own abilities to break through.*

ACTION STEP:

DANCING TIP 11 / Seek out a dance coach or expert and ask for specific feedback on what you can improve. Focus your request on things you can potentially fix on your own by practicing at home or at the studio. To receive a complimentary "Selecting the Perfect Coach" checklist, email us at info@nextleveldancing.com.

COACHING TIP 11 / Get used to receiving feedback by asking people whom you love and care about to offer you specific, measurable criticism. Most people are not trained to offer constructive remarks so give them some parameters. For example, you may want to ask them, "If I could change one thing to communicate or interact more effectively with you, what would it be?" or "What one trait do you think holds me back from getting what I want?" These are examples of questions that provide very specific information that you could do something with. Avoid asking things like "What are my biggest flaws?" or "What do you think I need to change about myself?" As the saying goes, "Be careful what you ask for."

"I WILL...."

STEP 3 / BEWARE OF THE DARK SIDE

"EVERYTHING THAT WE SEE IS A **SHADOW** CAST BY THAT WHICH WE DO NOT SEE."

— MARTIN LUTHER KING JR.

One of the concepts I introduce to my clients when we do behavioral development is the "dark side" or the "shadow." The term "shadow behavior" was coined by the esteemed Swiss psychiatrist Carl Jung to refer to negative or less favorable behaviors. We all have them, and they tend to appear during times of increased stress, pressure, or tension. As you go through Stage 3 and challenge yourself by asking for performance feedback from people you admire, you may see your shadows—such as defensiveness, resistance, or argumentativeness—show up if the feedback isn't favorable.

Some people are more aware of their shadows than others. The key to managing shadows is to acknowledge, accept, and work with them. **Shadows are directly connected to our strengths.** When we overextend them, they move from being positive to negative traits. For example, one of my strengths is that I am direct. This allows me to have clear communications in my business and dancing relationships. This same strength, however, when overused, can show up as blunt, aggressive, or insensitive, preventing me from connecting successfully with others. My job isn't to discredit these shadows. It is to learn to manage them so they don't become barriers to communication.

As we develop in our dancing and learn how to interact effectively with our instructors and coaches, we can benefit greatly from doing some shadow work. Don't worry if the concept of the shadow doesn't make complete sense to you at this point. Initially, it can be difficult to identify and come up with specific shadows in ourselves. If you struggle to find the right behaviors, ask someone you know really well and who loves you to share one behavior they see you exhibiting that could be a shadow. It may be helpful to ask: "What one negative or less favorable behavior do you see in me that you don't think I'm especially aware of?" Or, "If you could share one behavior that I seem to have less insight about, what would it be?" Remember, the purpose of asking these questions is to give you additional insight and awareness. After the person offers you feedback, kindly thank him or her and process the information. Are you surprised by what was shared? Do you see this shadow in yourself? Even if you don't agree, is there some merit to the feedback? The trick with shadows is that often we can't see ours as clearly as other people can, and we tend to be a bit defensive about them. If this happens as you ask for shadow feedback, chances are there is some truth to the information.

SELF-REFLECTIVE EXERCISE:

1. In one column, list at least five strengths that help you to be effective with others. List a possible shadow for each in the next column. For example, your strengths may be that you are open, honest, supportive, passionate, and persuasive. The corresponding shadows could be emotional (open), inappropriate (honest), controlling (supportive), intense (passionate), and self-promoting (persuasive). Record any insight, thoughts, or feelings in the last column.

STRENGTH	SHADOW (Strengths overextended)	INSIGHT

2. Pick one of your shadows that is standing in your way.

EXPERT ADVICE:

DAVID BUTCHER IS AN ASSOCIATE MEMBER OF THE IMPERIAL SOCIETY OF TEACHERS OF DANCING (ISTD), LATIN AND BALLROOM. HE SERVED ON THE ARTHUR MURRAY DANCE BOARD, AND IS A COACH AND INSTRUCTOR. HE WAS IN THE TOP THREE OF THE AMERICAN STYLE PRO CHAMPIONSHIP AND WAS A THEATER ARTS PRO/AM CHAMPION. HE LIVES IN COLUMBUS, OHIO.

JF: David, you are an experienced competitive dancer, adjudicator, and coach. How has the concept of "shadow behaviors" come in to play in your teaching or coaching? How have you helped students move past their "shadows" or negative behaviors to break through to the next level in their dancing?

DAVID: *Teaching dance has a lot less to do with introducing steps and techniques and more to do with interacting and communicating effectively with people. Sometimes I think I should have gone to school to be a therapist instead of a theater arts performer! Every dancer comes to dancing for a different reason. As an instructor and coach, my job is to tap in to those reasons and draw out the best in each person.*

Dancing is an emotional sport. It brings out the best—and sometimes the worst—in both the instructor and the dancer. Teachers must first learn how to handle their own shadows before they can effectively help their students move through theirs. At one point in my teaching, I realized that I was too similar to one of my top students, and we kept hitting a wall in our dancing. Our shadows included being stubborn, emotional, and volatile, and it was a recipe for disaster. In the end, we each asked the studio owner for help and came up with a plan that worked for both of us.

The key ingredient to help students move past their shadows is listening effectively to them—not just to what they say, but also to what they aren't saying. I sometimes have to remind myself that a student is being emotional, fearful, or abrasive for a reason. If I can tap in to that underlying cause by listening, I can get to the core issue and resolve it with my student.

Students can use this same technique by taking a few minutes to consider where an emotion is coming from and realizing that they can choose to change it. The instructor and student who can effectively maneuver around their shadows will have much more success and will enjoy their dancing more by creating a relationship based on trust and confidence.

JF: What tips or tools would you recommend for students whose negative behaviors stand in the way of them reaching their dancing goals?

DAVID: *Work with your instructor. Share your feelings outside the studio over coffee or at a time when you are no longer emotional. Listen to each other's responses to the shadows and be willing to work out the problem together. If you can't address it effectively in this way, ask for help from someone who is objective. Often another professional at the studio or a coach can offer additional insights. Take responsibility for your own actions and emotions. Shadows really can hold you back. Don't let them.*

ACTION STEP:

DANCING TIP 12 / Identify one of your most destructive shadow behaviors that affects your dancing progress negatively and write an action step for managing it more effectively. For example, you may fall into blaming behaviors when you are challenged. An action step that is effective when dealing with this particular shadow is to ask the other person what you can do differently to reach the next level. Taking personal ownership helps the blaming shadow behavior diminish.

COACHING TIP 12 / Shadows are not limited to the dance floor. They sneak up on you in every part of your life, and they love to rear their ugly heads during times when you are stressed. Identify a specific shadow that you tend to exhibit during stressful times. One of mine (and a common one for dominant individuals) is to verbally attack when I feel challenged. My counter shadow strategy is to be quiet, to not interrupt the other person, and to take at least three deep breaths before responding to the situation. I have learned to identify the energy before the shadow is in full bloom, which helps me control it. Remember, you can't eliminate your shadows, but you can learn to manage them more effectively.

"I WILL...."

PUSHING

CHAPTER 5:

THROUGH STAGE 4

"I BEGAN TO LEARN HOW TO DISTINGUISH BETWEEN THOSE WHO **KNEW THINGS** AND COULD SAY THEM, AND THOSE WHO COULD DO THOSE THINGS AND **BE THEM**."

— RICHARD STROZZI HECKLER

The wonders of Stage 4 are often subtle and gradual. A step or a moment that we spent days, weeks, or months practicing seems suddenly to appear effortlessly. If asked by others how we do it, we may not even be able to answer, because it's become muscle memory without our realizing it.

The truth is that it took a lot of hard work and repetition to get to Stage 4, and the beauty of dancing is that our practice is never over. **We don't "arrive" at a place where we can all of a sudden rely on our accumulated skills and talents.** Exceptional dancers never stop practicing, adjusting, or developing.

STEP 1 / PICK A DANCE, STEP, MOVEMENT, OR CHOREOGRAPHY AND FINE-TUNE IT

"EXCELLENCE IS A BETTER TEACHER THAN MEDIOCRITY. THE LESSONS OF THE ORDINARY ARE EVERYWHERE. TRULY PROFOUND AND ORIGINAL INSIGHTS ARE TO BE FOUND ONLY IN STUDYING THE EXEMPLARY."

— WARREN G. BENNIS

I love to work on and practice small and concise movements. My favorite dances are the waltz and rumba, and while these dances are very different in mood and technique, I refer to them as my "Powerpuff dances." The reference is to the anime Powerpuff Girls, who shoot up into the air with power and energy. When I conjure a depiction of them, I immediately see myself taking flight and moving straight up to my next level of performance.

Although the waltz and the rumba may not technically be my best dances, they make me feel graceful, powerful, and connected. So when I'm in Stage 4, these are the dances I choose to explore because they build confidence and remind me of why I love dancing.

SELF-REFLECTIVE EXERCISE:

1. Which dances bring you the most joy, confidence, and/or encouragement?

2. What can you do with that dance or those dances to sharpen and develop?

EXPERT ADVICE:

JACKIE ROGERS IS A CHAMPIONSHIP ADJUDICATOR IN ALL STYLES, A WORLD CHAMPIONSHIP MASTER SCRUTINEER, CHAMPIONSHIP CHAIRMAN OF JUDGES, AND A CERTIFIED FITNESS INSTRUCTOR WITH THE AMERICAN COLLEGE OF SPORTS MEDICINE. ROGERS ALSO CHOREOGRAPHED FOUR HALF-TIME SHOWS FOR THE GIANTS FOOTBALL TEAM, DEPLOYING MORE THAN 210 TEACHERS AND STUDENTS IN A 10-MINUTE AEROBIC FORMATION PRESENTATION TWICE ON MONDAY NIGHT FOOTBALL. SHE RESIDES BETWEEN LAKE ARIEL, PA., AND PORT ST. LUCIE, FLA.

JF: You have been involved in dancing at several different levels for most of your life. What is one important lesson that you have learned about perfecting your technique or process?

JACKIE: *I love to dance, but I think I will use another sport to illustrate this point. In addition to dancing, I have been playing tennis since I was a young girl. I've gotten pretty good at it, and I am used to and comfortable with my one-handed backhand. As I evolve in my game and as I get older, I need to learn to use a two-handed backhand to take my game to the next level. The challenge is that I'm very comfortable using a one-handed backhand, and I know I can score well when I use it. I also know that if I don't elevate my game by replacing the one-handed with a two-handed backhand, I won't do well in the future. Sometimes you have to be willing to let go of something that works well and that you are comfortable with in order to raise your game.*

This is not a particularly fun process. It's painful, both physically and ego-wise. When I have doubt or feel insecure, my tennis coach reminds me that it's better to try the two-handed backhand and miss the point rather than continue to use the old one-handed backhand that helps me now, so I can be the type of player I desire.

JF: What piece of advice would you give dancers relating to developing and taking their dancing to the next level?

JACKIE: *Remember that dancing is a graceful and elegant sport. It is important, for both social and competitive dancers, to practice being graceful on and off the dance floor. Honor this sport by dressing and acting with class at all times. Treat others the way you would like to be treated and be a good steward of the sport.*

ACTION STEP:

DANCING TIP 13 / Conduct a "fine-tuning audit" of your dancing. Commit to one action that will help you take your dancing to the next level. Pick a specific step that you want to improve. Set aside at least 45 minutes and practice only that move. Consider every muscle and movement as you repeat the step over and over. Notice what you are learning about yourself and your body. Is there a part that offers resistance, or are there parts that move effortlessly? Take notes after the exercise and ask for feedback about your progress from your instructor or coach.

COACHING TIP 13 / Developing excellence in a particular area requires focus and dedication. In what part of your life would you like to develop excellence? It could be a particular part of your job, your role as a parent, or as a friend. It may be that you want to develop your follow-up skills and commit to always returning phone calls within 24 hours or to set aside a specific amount of time to connect with important friends and family members at least once per week. Once you develop a habit of doing something well and without flaw, excellence flows naturally.

"I WILL...."

STEP 2 / FIND A DANCE MENTOR (LIVING, DEAD, NEAR OR FAR)

"I HAVE NEVER STUDIED WITH BALANCHINE, BUT HIS WORK IS VERY IMPORTANT TO ME."

— TWYLA THARP

Twyla Tharp, world renowned contemporary dance chorographer and Emmy and Tony Award winner, speaks about her mentor in the Harvard Business Review Article, "Creativity Step by Step." She refers to George Balanchine, the brilliant artistic director of the New York City Ballet, as her "invisible mentor." She was never able to study with him directly because he didn't offer classes or coaching lessons to outsiders. Instead, she spent more than 20 years trying to learn from him by mentally parking him in a corner of her studio, pretending to see her own work through his eyes. Her advice about finding a mentor goes as follows:

> Just go to Barnes & Noble and pull down a book from the shelf— pick out a writer, pick out a thinker. Pick out somebody who can teach you something, not somebody who's going to sit down and gossip with you. Do you want somebody to hold your hand, or do you want to learn something? If you want to learn, go for it—end of story.

My professional dance mentor is Bree Watson, and she had no idea how much she inspired me until recently. When I first met her, I was in awe of her and approaching her seemed too daunting. Instead, I watched and studied her. I attempted to move like her, and I observed how she interacted on and off the dance floor. I was struck by her grace, beauty, and dance technique. As I have gotten to know her, I'm continually impressed with her kindness, generosity, hard work, and competitive spirit.

When I took my first coaching lesson with Bree I asked her how she has developed such a distinct rumba walk. I was expecting a special technique or strategy, but instead she said, "I just practice it over and over and over and over again." Of course! **There is no miracle solution to dancing.**

It reminded me that **it is hard work, persistence, and perseverance that make a top dancer.** While she is an exceptionally talented dancer, she has to work hard—just like all the rest of us—to produce extraordinary results. My dance partner and I have since coined the term "Breewalks" instead of rumba walks, which reminds us that they don't just appear naturally!

I also have an amateur competitive dance mentor. She is a fantastic dancer who does amazingly well in all of the styles in which she competes. You can almost see the other competitors' disappointed looks when they realize she is competing in their heats. She is just that good! What I admire most about her is her obvious commitment to her dancing and level of excellence. She is technically impressive and maintains fantastic showmanship on the dance floor. She is a force to be reckoned with and I admire her unfalteringly composed attitude.

A dance mentor, professional or amateur, will inspire you on many levels. You may even be surprised to know that at some point in your dance journey you may have become someone else's mentor. That is another reason why it is always important to maintain a positive and encouraging attitude on and off the dance floor.

SELF-REFLECTIVE EXERCISE:

1. What dancer inspires you and why? It can be an amateur or a professional dancer, judge, choreographer. Don't worry about if they are alive or dead, or are close or far.

_____
_____
_____
_____
_____

2. What is it about this person that you admire? Use adjectives to describe him or her.

_____
_____
_____
_____
_____

3. If you had a chance to meet or interact with this person, what would you ask to reach your dancing goals?

_____
_____
_____
_____
_____

EXPERT ADVICE:

JEFFREY GOLTIAO IS A PROFESSIONAL DANCE INSTRUCTOR IN COLUMBUS, OHIO.

JF: Not only are you a great dancer, but you are truly an exceptional teacher. What person has inspired you most in your dance career and why?

JEFFREY: *Without question, Sam Sodano. I was looking for a mentor who would inspire me to be great at my craft but also great with people. Sam personifies that for me. He is confident, doesn't doubt himself, and believes in himself and his teaching methods completely. He goes out of his way to help everyone in the ballroom world, from amateurs and professionals to sponsors and vendors. He knows everyone's name, and he makes people feel like they really matter. I strive to be that kind of person in the ballroom world.*

JF: What two tips would you offer to dancers who are seeking a mentor?

JEFFREY: *Indentify your dancing goal and look for top performers— amateurs and professionals—who align with your goals. Study them and watch how they act on and off the dance floor. Remember, there is a fine line between studying someone and stalking them. Be courteous and sensitive to their personal space. It is more important to learn from them by observation than getting to know them personally.*

Pick someone you would be proud to represent. A mentor is someone who inspires you to be the best version of yourself. Carefully select someone who you feel you would be proud to represent. For me, it isn't enough for a mentor to be a great dancer. They have to also be a great person.

ACTION STEP:

DANCING TIP 14 / Select a dance mentor (living or dead, near or far) and study that person. What are/were they doing that you like? What attributes would you like to emulate? Write down the specific things you wish to work on and begin practicing. If you are fortunate enough to connect with that person, let them know how and why they inspire you and ask for their advice on how to grow as a dancer.

COACHING TIP 14 / Find a life mentor or hire a coach you admire to help you to develop in every part of life. Mentors can come in all shapes and sizes and tend to appear where you least expect them. One of my most influential mentors was my ex-boyfriend's mother. She gave me a key life lesson. She told me to move forward and discover myself instead of focusing on trying to fix other people. She helped me to see that we all have a journey and that it isn't our job to push other people along on their paths to meet our agendas. I know she came into my life for a reason. Today, as an executive coach, being neutral and objective in helping other people reach their goals is a key attribute to being great at what I do.

A life or business coach is someone who actively helps you reach your goals. Before becoming a coach myself, I hired a coach to help me reorganize my life in to the one that I desired. To achieve this, I knew that I had to end an unsatisfying relationship and leave an unfulfilling job and that I wanted a dog. Today, I live the life I always dreamed of and my little Scottish Terrier Mac is almost nine years old. In short, mentors and coaches propel you forward. As the saying goes, "When the student is ready, the teacher appears." Are you ready? For a complimentary article on selecting a life or business coach, please email me at jessika@nextleveldancing.com.

"I WILL...."

STEP 3 / TAKE A BREAK TO RECHARGE AND REENERGIZE YOUR BODY AND SOUL

"TAKE REST; A FIELD THAT HAS **RESTED** GIVES A BOUNTIFUL CROP."

— OVID

When you reach Stage 4, you experience a certain sense of calmness. All of a sudden, you don't have to struggle so much and things seem to flow naturally. This is the perfect time to take a break! Experienced athletes and coaches know that the body needs time to rest and the mind needs time to process.

As a new dancer with ambitious goals, I remember thinking that taking three weeks off without dancing would derail me so dramatically that I couldn't possibly recover. I thought I would lose my edge, and it would take months to get back to where I left off.

The more I learn about myself as a person and about my dancing, the more I realize that these are just my fears talking. I'm actually on a four-week dancing break as I'm typing this, **and I have found that taking a physical, emotional, and mental break helps me to propel faster and with more joy.** I'm always amazed that, after I emerge from a short time off, people comment on my dancing, asking what new strategy or skill I have been doing to push my dancing forward. They are equally surprised when my answer is that I took a break.

While taking a physical dance break can produce important results, taking a mental or emotional pause does even more. In our hectic, multitasking lives, we are constantly inundated with information. This overstimulation of our senses creates an internal buzz that is hard to silence.

One of my professional mentors, Barbara Braham, takes a month off each year and stays silent to quiet her mind and to reach her full potential. That may seem extreme to some. When I asked her how she ended up taking off an entire month, she said, "I started with just a few hours and worked my way up." The famous self-help guru and author Deepak Chopra encourages people to take a few minutes a day to sit silently to allow for creative thoughts to emerge. He also warns his readers that when you first start a sitting exercise or quite mediation, your brains doesn't make it easy for you. Your thoughts tend to flutter all over the place, and you may find it hard to focus. I have mediated for more than 10 years, and I still find it challenging at times. But every now and then, I hit that place where my mind empties and I'm completely present. I usually emerge after that kind of mediation with increased clarity, rekindled passion, and an internal assuredness that I'm on the right path. Through repetitive silent or meditative practices, I find the increased self-confidence, calmness, and balance I need to advance my dancing to the next stage.

Most lifelong dancers have a system or way for balancing. They have learned the hard way that not taking time out to reenergize can have disastrous results.

SELF-REFLECTIVE EXERCISE:

1. What are your biggest fears about taking time away from dancing?

_____
_____
_____
_____
_____

2. What benefits could you experience by taking some time off?

_____
_____
_____
_____
_____

3. On the scale below, please rate your dance/life balance (1=completely out of balance, 10=perfectly balanced).

```
       +                                    -
      10   9   8   7   6   5   4   3   2   1
```

If you scored a 7 or below, chances are that you could benefit from a mini break and some type of balancing activity. If you scored 8 or above, chances are that you already have a system for balancing your dancing and your life.

4. If you scored below a 7, what type of balancing activity could you benefit from? Some examples include daily mini-meditations, a few days away from dancing, and designated quiet time.

_____

_____

_____

_____

5. If you scored 8 or above, what balancing activity that you already engage in could you do more of or more frequently for an added benefit?

_____

_____

_____

_____

EXPERT ADVICE:

BECCI AND BARRY BERNARD ARE PRO/AM AND AM/AM COMPETITORS, BALLROOM ENTREPRENEURS, AND DANCESPORT ENTHUSIASTS FROM CINCINNATI, OHIO.

JF: Becci and Barry, you just returned from a 10-year dancing break and redefined how dancing would fit into your lives. What were some of the most challenging and rewarding experiences about the break and the return to dancing?

BARRY: At one point in our dancing careers, we both taught, owned a dance studio, and lived the ballroom lifestyle 24/7. One day we realized that we had missed out on almost every important family event and that dancing had started to consume us. So we took a break to figure out what we wanted to do with our lives and careers. All of a sudden, we realized that 10 years had gone by, and we began to miss the physical, emotional, and creative benefits of dancing. Now that we have returned to dancing, we are having more fun and are more balanced. We recognized that one of our shadows as a couple was that we can give up too much for our dancing passions if we aren't balanced. This time around, we have a greater sense of what we need in our lives to prevent dance burnout, and we are actually having a lot more fun.

BECCI: When we took our break, I ended up gaining a lot of weight. Plus, I had two surgeries that took a long time to recover from. I became really hard on myself, and my confidence took a hit. I needed to lose the weight and get back to being healthy, so I re-introduced dancing into my life. Initially, it was hard getting back in to it and putting myself back out there. But it's been interesting to return to dancing now that I don't have to do it for a living. Prior to taking the break, I was so concerned about how we looked and what people and judges would think about our dancing. I would say that my biggest weakness back then was that I cared too much about other people's opinions, and I was overly concerned about how our dancing would reflect on our business. Now that dancing is a hobby and not my profession anymore, I am much freer to just dance and share my love for dancing without any hesitation or care."

JF: What tips or tools would you offer dancers who have taken a break and may have fears or self-limiting beliefs that hold them back?

BARRY: *There are so many benefits to dancing. When you emerge from a break, you have clearer insight about the fact that dancing keeps you in physical shape, clears your thinking, and offers you challenging mental stimulation. In my case, taking the break enabled me to get clear about my priorities, and where I used to have insecurities and doubt about my dancing, I now have confidence and assuredness. The difference is that I just don't care anymore what other people think. I remind myself that I do this because I love it. If we can always remind ourselves of that, a lot of our fears will dissipate.*

BECCI: *Remember to reconnect with why you love to dance. Remind yourself that your dancing is connected to a bigger picture. Also, if you don't dance professionally, you probably have a lot of other priorities to manage. It's important to remember as an amateur dancer that there is only so much time to get so good. There is no use beating yourself up trying to be as good as a professional when you have only a couple of hours a week to dedicate to your dancing.*

ACTION STEP:

DANCING TIP 15 / Schedule a mini break. Set aside a few days and avoid any contact with dance-related activities or thoughts. I know. This is not as easy as it sounds. Should you feel yourself sliding back, regroup and get back on track. Don't judge yourself; simply begin again. After your break, reflect on the experience. Do you feel more focused, relaxed, or energized? What challenging feelings and emotions appeared? How can you incorporate mini breaks into your dancing to continue to experience these benefits?

COACHING TIP 15 / Incorporate mini breaks throughout every part of your life. Get used to setting boundaries in order to take time off. For example, let people in your life and work know that you will be taking a break and will not be responding to phone calls, emails, or other requests. Start small with an afternoon or a day off and gradually work your way up to a significant amount of time that will truly recharge you. Or commit to doing it more often. Once people get used to you taking time off, they will give you the space you need to recharge and focus on yourself.

I remember the first time I told my clients that I was taking a month off and wouldn't be responding to email or calls. I was terrified! What if they decided to leave me? What if they thought I was irresponsible? Well, my fears quickly dissipated as all my clients supported me and were actually jealous of my ability to set boundaries and take time off. As my competing takes up a lot of time, I now take a few weeks off each year instead of a solid month. But my clients still know that when I'm off dancing, I won't respond to texts and emails. The key to successfully taking time off is to prepare those around you and then stick with your plan. It's easy to get sucked in to checking and responding. Avoid it at all costs. You need your time off.

"I WILL...."

THE DANCING EXPERTS
SHORT

CHAPTER 6:

KEEP IT
AND SWEET

"TO DANCE IS TO BE OUT OF YOURSELF. LARGER, MORE BEAUTIFUL, MORE POWERFUL."

— AGNES DE MILLE

We are blessed to have such amazing talent in our ballroom community. Here is a short summary of the tips each expert offered in this book. You may find it helpful to keep one or a few of these tips handy as you move along your dancing journey. Remember that an informal mentor or a powerful quote can inspire you to reach new levels of performance and enjoyment in your dancing.

BONITA BROKERT: "Many things correct themselves as you go, and knowing what to focus on at what time is crucial to avoiding the "stuck" place, which is so frustrating. Many dancers try to emulate a "look" or product, not understanding that the process and understanding of mechanics and musicality will eventually produce the right look."

PAMELA BOLLING: "If you want to continue to dance, you have to look internally for motivation and not worry about what other people think of you. It is easy to get caught up in trying to please other people, but the truth is that the only person who has to be happy with your dancing is you."

BILL SPARKS: "Dancing is a high-energy sport, and it pushes your emotions and feelings."

MAUREEN ANDREWS: "Build a network of amateur dancers. Talk to other students to get support, encouragement, and feedback."

IZABELLA JUNDZILL: "Figure out one thing that you do really well or better than most other people. Consider all aspects of your life when identifying your unique gifts. What motivates us in life tends to be what motivates us to dance."

RON CLARK: "The way I look at it, obstacles are only patterns that reappear in your life. How you handle them is what matters most."

LINDA CARPENTER: "Listen to your instructor when he or she gives you positive feedback."

KRISTEN WHEELER: "Be specific about what your favorite part of dancing is—not what parts of dancing you're good at, but what parts make you light up. It might be invisible to you, so consider asking a trusted observer of your dancing."

PIERRE ALLAIRE: "Make good use of mirrors. Pick a movement or step and exaggerate the motion. Do you look in the mirror the way you picture yourself in your mind? Is the reflection in the mirror how you want to look? If not, what changes do you need to make to reach the next level?"

MIREILLE VEILLEUX: "Dancing is always about working on the fundamentals. Sometimes, the higher we get in our dancing, the easier it is to forget about the basics. If you are getting frustrated or emotional because you can't push through to the next level, go back and work on the basics you already know."

BRENDAN DONELSON: "I encourage any amateur men to dance with other amateur women to see what they are not doing/leading."

CHRISTINA DONELSON: "Instead of observing those in your skill level or age category, observe the dancers in more advanced categories. This will inspire you rather than discourage you."

DECHO KRAEV: "I'll keep it short. You have to love what you do and do what you love."

BREE WATSON: "Remember that going beyond just "good" or "good enough" will bring great rewards. You may find that by pushing yourself beyond what you currently think you can do enables you to grow both as a dancer and a person."

SAM SODANO: "Don't listen to naysayers who don't believe in your goals. Align yourself with people who are supportive and positive."

DAVID BUTCHER: "Take responsibility for your own actions and emotions. Shadows really can hold you back. Don't let them."

JACKIE ROGERS: *"Remember that dancing is a graceful and elegant sport. It is important, for both social and competitive dancers, to practice being graceful on and off the dance floor."*

JEFFREY GOLTIAO: *"A mentor is someone who inspires you to be the best version of yourself. Carefully select someone who you feel you would be proud to represent."*

BARRY BERNARD: *"When you emerge from a break, you have clearer insight about the fact that dancing keeps you in physical shape, clears your thinking, and offers you challenging mental stimulation".*

BECCI BERNARD: *"There is no use beating yourself up trying to be as good as a professional when you have only a couple of hours a week to dedicate to your dancing."*

CHAPTER 7:

SUMMING IT UP

"IN THE LIFE OF THE SPIRIT THERE IS NO ENDING THAT IS NOT A BEGINNING."

— HENRIETTA SZOLD

This book started as a bunch of notes in my dancing folder. When I first began to dance, I couldn't find resources that would help me take my dancing to the next level. While there are great books about other people's dancing journeys and authors' evaluations of the ballroom dancing world, I couldn't find resources that were tactical enough to help me work through the physical and emotional stages I was experiencing. I often felt alone and believed that I was the only one going through these feelings and emotions.

As I built my dancing network and began to talk to my fellow dancers, I realized that I wasn't alone at all and that amateurs and professionals are all going through the exact same process (over and over again). That was when I knew this book had to be written.

While I have now graduated from a "baby" to an "adolescent" dancer, according to my dance coach Bonita Brokert, I'm far from a dancing expert. I am, however, a master-level executive coach, and I knew that if I could combine my skills as a business coach with the expert advice of professional and amateur dancers, organizers, and judges, I could create a book that offered something unique to the dance community. It is my hope that this book is just the first in a series that will offer hands-on tools and techniques to help take you from the dancer you are to the dancer you see in your dreams. You can also access other dancing resources on our web site at **http://www.nextleveldancing.com**.

It has been a pleasure sharing these concepts and exercises with you, and I hope that you seek me out in the ballroom dancing world to share what has worked for you as you reach your dancing goals. Don't forget to complete your action plan outlined in the next couple of pages. Remember, nothing will be different if you don't do something differently.

With love,

CHAPTER 8:

MOVING INTO ACTION

"ACTION IS THE FOUNDATIONAL KEY TO ALL SUCCESS."

— PABLO PICASSO

At this point, you have learned a lot about yourself, your dancing goals, and how to take your dancing to the next level. This chapter summarizes your action steps to move you forward. Remember, increased awareness is important, but nothing will change unless you change your actions.

LETS GET STARTED...

TAKING MY DANCING TO THE NEXT LEVEL
ACTION PLAN

CHAPTER 1 / THE NATURAL STAGES OF CHANGE

1. I'm currently at Stage _____ in my dancing, and I wholeheartedly embrace this stage knowing that I'm here because I'm about to transform in my dancing.

2. To help me get through this stage, I'm committing to the following action steps:

→ _____
→ _____
→ _____
→ _____

CHAPTER 2 / GETTING THROUGH STAGE 2— THE FIRST TIME

1. The reason I dance is:

_____
_____
_____

2. The most challenging feeling about where I currently am is:

_____
_____
_____

3. I'm most proud of the following dance skill:

_____
_____
_____
_____

4. The following affirmation statement keeps me focused and positive about my dancing:

_____
_____
_____
_____

CHAPTER 3 / GETTING THROUGH STAGE 2—OVER AND OVER AND OVER AGAIN

1. I will do the following to remind myself that I've been here before:

_____
_____
_____
_____

2. My most destructive gremlin is:

_____
_____
_____
_____

3. Next time it appears, I will:

4. My inner coach would give me the following advice when I feel down or defeated:

5. My biggest strength as a dancer is:

6. I will commit to doing the following to maximize my strength(s):

7. One of my weaknesses as a dancer is:

8. I will do the following to avoid over focusing on this weakness:

_____
_____
_____
_____

9. I will do the following to avoid being overly reliant on my feelings and emotions while at Stage 2:

_____
_____
_____
_____

10. I dance because:

_____
_____
_____
_____

11. I will do the following to remind me that my journey is unique, and I will not compare myself to others:

_____
_____
_____
_____

CHAPTER 4 / EMBRACING STAGE 3

1. I commit to practicing or doing the following at least three times in the next two weeks to sharpen my dancing:

_____

_____

_____

_____

2. I will ask the following person for honest feedback about my dancing (even if I have to pay a coach or professional for it):

_____

_____

_____

_____

3. I am aware of the following shadow behavior that may stand in my way of my dancing success:

_____

_____

_____

_____

4. I will take the following action step to manage it more effectively:

_____

_____

_____

_____

CHAPTER 5: PUSHING THROUGH STAGE 4

1. I will explore the following movement, dance step, or choreography over the next week:

_____

_____

_____

_____

2. When I'm done, I expect to see the following result:

_____

_____

_____

_____

3. My dance mentor is:

_____

_____

_____

4. I admire him or her because:

_____

_____

_____

_____

5. I will practice or do the following to emulate his or her behavior/dance technique/skill/attitude:

_____
_____
_____

6. I will do the following to ensure that I am balanced and take time off to recharge:

_____
_____
_____
_____

CHAPTER 6 / THE DANCING EXPERTS KEEP IT SHORT AND SWEET

1. I found the following quote from Chapter 6 especially inspiring/motivating/encouraging:

_____
_____
_____
_____

IF I DO NOTHING ELSE WITH THIS MATERIAL, I WILL AT LEAST:

RESOURCES AND REFERENCES

BOOKS:

THE ALCHEMIST by Paulo Coelho

THE ANATOMY OF CHANGE: *East/West Approaches to Body/Mind Therapy* by Richard Strozzi Heckler

A YEAR OF DANCING DANGEROUSLY: *One Woman's Journey from Beginner to Winner* by Lydia Raurell

BALLROOM DANCING IS NOT FOR SISSIES: *An R-Rated Guide for Partnership* by Elizabeth A. Seagull & Arthur A. Seagull

BODY MIND MASTERY: *Creating Success in Sport and Life* by Dan Millman

THE CREATIVE HABIT: *Learn It and Use It for Life* by Twyla Tharp

DANCING THROUGH LIFE by Antoinette Benevento with Edwin Dobb

FEEL THE FEAR AND DO IT ANYWAY by Susan J. Jeffers

GOOD TO GREAT: *Why Some Companies Make the Leap...and Others Don't* by Jim Collins

GLAMOUR ADDICTION: *Inside the American Ballroom Dance Industry* by Juliet McMains

NOW DISCOVER YOUR STRENGTHS by Marcus Buckingham and Donald O. Clifton

TAMING YOUR GREMLIN: *A Guide to Enjoying Yourself* by Richard D. Carson

THE SEVEN SPIRITUAL LAWS OF SUCCESS by Deepak Chopra

STRENGTHS-BASED LEADERSHIP by Tom Rath and Barry Conchie

WAY OF THE PEACEFUL WARRIOR by Dan Millman

WEBSITES:

For more information on the **"STAGES OF LEARNING AND CHANGE"**:
http://www.businessballs.com/consciouscompetencelearningmodel.htm

Concepts from **"GOOD TO GREAT"**: http://www.jimcollins.com

Music by **TEMPLETON THOMPSON**:
http://www.templetonthompson.com/fr_home.cfm

ARTICLES:

"**CREATIVITY STEP BY STEP**: A Conversation with Choreographer,"
Twyla Tharp, Harvard Business Review, Reprint R0804B, April 2008

COMPETITIONS:

For those of you who wish to explore competing, below is a list of the most popular ballroom competitions in alphabetical order, as listed by DanceSport Competitions. You can find more information about all things ballroom-related on the website at http://dancesportcompetitions.com/

The following listing shares the dates for each competition for 2010 and 2011. Google competitions you are interested in attending to learn more and to verify dates.
AAU - ALHC National Dance Championships, Stamford, Conn.
American Star Ball Championships, Bellmawr, N.J.
Atlanta Open Dancesport Competition, Atlanta, Ga.
Atlantic Dancesport Challenge, Baltimore, Md.
BYU Dancesport Championships, Provo, Utah
Baltimore Dance Challenge & Showcase, College Park, Md.
Berkeley Ballroom Classic, Berkeley, Calif.
Berkeley Ballroom Beginners Comp, Berkeley, Calif.
Big Apple Dance Festival, New York, N.Y.
Big Apple Dancesport Challenge, New York, N.Y.
Binghamton Ballroom Dance Revolution, Binghamton, N.Y.
Blackpool Dance Festival, Blackpool, England

Boston University Terrier Dancesport, Boston, Mass.
California Open Champs, Irvine, Calif.
California Star Ball Champs, Costa Mesa, Calif.
Cal-Poly Mustang Ball, San Luis Obispo, Calif.
Canada DanceSport, Kingston, Ontario, Canada
Capital Dancesport, Washington D.C./Alexandria, Va.
Cardinal Classic Dancesport, Stanford, Calif.
Caribbean Dancesport Classic, San Juan, Puerto Rico
Carolina Classic Competition, Greensboro, N.C.
Carolina Fall Classic, Greensboro, N.C.
Charlotte Dancesport Challenge, Charlotte, N.C.
Chicago Dancesport Challenge Champs, Chicago, Ill.
Chicago Crystal Ball, Chicago, Ill.
Chicago Harvest Moon Ball Championship, Chicago, Ill.
City Lights Ball, San Francisco, Calif.
Cleveland Dancesport Challenge, Cleveland, Ohio
Colorado Star Ball, Denver, Colo.
Columbia Star Ball, Portland, Ore.
Commonwealth Classic, Lowell, Mass.
Constitution State Challenge, Stamford, Conn.
Costa Rica Open Dancesport, San Jose, Costa Rica
Costa Rican Classic, San Jose, Costa Rica
Crown Jewel Of Dancesport, Miami Beach, Fla.
Crystal Ball Dance Competitions, Chicago, Ill.
Crystal Leaf Canadian Open Dancesport, Toronto, Ontario, Canada
DC Dance Challenge, Washington, D.C.
Dvida® National Dancesport, Las Vegas, Nev.
Dance Houston, Houston, Texas
Dance Vision Classic & Mastery Camp, Las Vegas. Nev.
Dancing A La Carte Champs, Springfield, Mass.
Dansesport Montreal, Montreal, Canada
Desert Classic Dancesport Festival, Palm Desert, Calif.
Desert Challenge Intercollegiate Champs, Las Vegas, Nev.
Disco America Dance Festival, Atlantic City, N.J.
Eastern United States Dancesport, Boston, Mass.
Easterns - Washington Dance Challenge, Washington, D.C.
Embassy Ball Dance Sport Championship, Irvine, Calif.

Emerald Ball Dancesport Championships, Los Angeles, Calif.
Empire State Dance Sport Champ, New York, N.Y.
Falls Premier Ball Niagara Falls, Ontario, Canada
Fire And Ice Dance Spectacular, Tampa, Fla.
First Coast Classic Dancesport, Jacksonville, Fla.
Florida State Dancesport, Sarasota, Fla.
Florida Superstars Dancesport, Tampa, Fla.
Galaxy Dancefest, Phoenix, Ariz.
Golden State Challenge, Newport Beach, Calif.
Grand National Shag Champs, Atlanta, Ga.
Grand National Dancesport, Miami Beach, Fla.
Grand Pacific Dance Champs, San Jose, Calif.
Gumbo Dancesport, Baton Rouge, La.
Halloween In Harrisburg©, Harrisburg, Pa.
Harvard Invitational Champs, Cambridge, Mass.
Hawaii Star Ball, Honolulu, Hawaii
Heart Of America Champs, Kansas City, Mo.
Heartland Classic, USA Dance, Indianapolis, Ind.
Heritage Classic Dancesport, Asheville, N.C.
High Desert Dancesport Classic, Lancaster, Calif.
High Point Classic Now Carolina Fall Classic,
 Greensboro-High Point,   N.C.
Hill Country Dance Classic, Austin, Texas
Holiday Ball & Dance Camp, San Francisco, Calif.
Holiday Dance Classic Champs, Las Vegas, Nev.
Hollywood Dancesport, Woodland Hills. Calif.
Holy Cross Ballroom Dance Competition, Worcester, Mass.
Hotlanta Dance Challenge, Atlanta, Ga.
IDSF 2011 World Senior 1 Ten Dance Champs, Toronto, Ontario, Canada
Indiana Challenge, Merriville, Ind.
Inter-state Dancesport Challenge, Mclean, Va.
International Grand Ball, San Francisco, Calif.
International Hustle & Salsa Competition, Miami, Fla.
International Lindy Hop Championships, Arlington, Va.
The Kings Ball, Staten Island, N.Y.
La Classique Du Québec, Montréal, Canada
Liberty Swing Dance Champs, New Brunswick, N.J.

MIT Open Competition, Cambridge, Mass.
Mid Atlantic Dance Jam (madjam), Tysons Corner, Va.
Magnolia Dancesport Challenge, Biloxi, Miss.
Manhattan Amateur Classic, New York City, N.Y.
Manhattan Dancesport, Manhattan, N.Y.
Maryland Dancesport Champs, Baltimore, Md.
Michigan Dance Challenge, Dearborn, Mich.
Mid-Atlantic Championships USA Dance, Bethesda, Md.
Midatlantic Dance Classic, Baltimore, Md.
Migrant Heritage Ballroom Dance Competiltion, Fairfax, Va.
Millennium 2000 Dancesport, St. Petersburg, Fla.
Mit Open Ballroom Competition, Cambridge, Mass.
Minnesota Star Ball Dance Competition, Minnetonka, Minn.
Music City Invitational, Nashville, Tenn.
Cal Poly Mustang Ball, San Luis Obispo, Calif.
Nashville Starz Dance Spectacular, Nashville, Tenn.
Neil Clover Ballroom Challenge, Princeton, N.J.
Neveda Star Ball, Las Vegas, Nev.
New England Fall Challenge, Glastonbury, Conn.
NJ Dancesport Spring Fling, Garfield, N.J.
NJ Dancesport Summer Sizzler ,West Orange, N.J.
NJ Dancesport Fall Frolci, Hackensack, N.J.
New Year's Dancin' Eve, Burlington, Mass.
New York Hustle Congress, New York, N.Y.
New York Dance Festival, New York, N.Y.
North American Dancesport Championships®, Indianapolis, Ind.
North Carolina Classic, Charlotte, N.C.
Northcoast Ballroom Championships, Cleveland, Ohio
Northeast Collegiate Dancesport Chall, Waltham, Mass.
Northeastern Open Inv. Dancesport, Stamford, Conn.
Northwest Regional Dancesport, Seattle, Wash.
Ohio Star Ball & Dancesport Superbowl, Columbus, Ohio
Pacific Dancesport Now Hollywood Dancesport, Woodland Hills, Calif.
Pacific Grand Ball ,Fremont, Calif.
People's Choice Dance-sport Competition, Scottsdale, Ariz.
Philadelphia Liberty Dance Challenge, Philadelphia, Pa.
Philadelphia Festival & Atlantic Coast Dancesport, Philadelphia, Pa.

Philadelphia Liberty Dance Challenge, Philadelphia, Pa.
Phoenix Dancesport Challenge, Phoenix, Ariz.
River City Ballroom Dance Competition, Richmond, Va.
Riverfront Dancesport Festival, Covington, Ky.
Rutgers Dancesport Competition, New Brunswick, N.J.
SJSU Ballroom Classic At, San Jose, Calif.
Salsa World Champs, Hollywood, Fla.
San Diego Dancesport Championships, San Diego, Calif.
San Francisco Open Champs, San Francisco, Calif.
San Francisco Open Dancesport, San Francisco, Calif.
San Francisco Open Dancesport, San Francisco, Calif.
San Francisco Autumn Dance Classic, San Francisco, Calif.
Sapphire Ball Dancesport Championships, Austin, Texas
Savannah Dance Classic, Savannah, Ga.
Seattle Star Ball, Seattle, Wash.
Snow Ball Classic DanceSport, Vancouver, Canada
Southeastern States Dancesport, SeaWorld, Fla.
Southern States Dancesport, New Orleans, La.
Southwestern Invitational Dancesport Champs, Dallas, Texas
Spring Dancesport Challenge, Stoney Creek, Ontario, Canada
St. Louis Star Ball ,St. Louis, Mo.
Stardust Open Dancesport, Atlantic City, N.J.
Sunshine State Dance Challenge, Ft Lauderdale, Fla.
Swing Fling, Washington, D.C.
Texas Challenge Dancesport, Houston, Texas
Three Rivers Ballroom Dance Challenge, Pittsburgh, Pa.
Tri-state Connection, Slyde, Competition, Vienna, Va.
Tri-State Challenge, Stamford, Conn.
Triangle Open Dancesport, Raleigh, N.C.
Tufts Ballroom Competition, Medford, Mass.
Twin Cities Open, Minneapolis, Minn.
Twin Cities Open Ballroom Championships, Minneapolis, Minn.
UCWDC Worlds Xix©, Nashville, Tenn.
US Open Swing Dance Champs, Anaheim, Calif.
USA Dance Chicago Dancesport Challenge, Chicago, Ill.
USA Dance Gumbo Dancesport, Baton Rouge, La.
USA Dance Heartland Classic, Indianapolis, Ind.

USA Dance Manhattan AM Classic, New York, N.Y.
USA Dance Mid-atlantic Champs, Bethesda, Md.
USA Dance National Dancesport, Baltimore, Md.
USA Dance Northwest Regionals, Seattle, Wash.
USA Dance Phoenix Dancesport, Phoenix, Ariz.
USA Dance Royal Palm Dancesport, Pompano Beach, Fla.
USA Dance Smoky Mountain Dancesport, Knoxville, Tenn.
United States Dance Champs, Orlando, Fla.
US Open Swing Dance Champs, San Jose, Calif.
Vegas Open Dance Challenge, Las Vegas, Nev.
Virginia State Dancesport Champs, Reston, Va.
Virginia State Open Pro Am Swing & Hustle Champs, Washington, D.C.
Volunteer State Dance Challenge, Nashville, Tenn.
Windy City Open Dancesport Competition, Chicago, Ill.
Wisconsin State Dancesport Champs, Milwaukee, Wis.
World Hustle Dance Champs, East Brunswick, N.J.
World Pro/Am Championships, Columbus, Ohio
World Prof Am Smooth & Rhythm Champs, Columbus, Ohio
World Swing Dance Championships, San Bernardino, Calif.
Yankee Classic Dancesport, Cambridge, Mass.
Yuletide Ball & Dancesport, Washington, D.C.

ABOUT THE AUTHOR

JESSIKA FERM is a master-level, award-winning executive coach. In the spring of 2009 she began ballroom dancing and her life has never been the same. During the day she runs a successful leadership development practice with offices in Columbus, OH, Boston, MA and Gothenburg, Sweden. Away from her business life, she is competitive amateur ballroom dancer who has been named the 2010 North American 9 and 6-Dance Champion and Best of the Best Participant representing the Atlanta Open at the 2010 Ohio Star Ball.

Jessika wrote the book The Ballroom Dance Coach: Expert Strategies To Take Your Dancing To the Next Level to help dancers go beyond sparkles and spray tans into the mindset techniques and action steps that can transform a hobbyist into a champion. In 2011, she created "Next Level Dancing," a company and online community that offers tools, advice, and services to the ballroom dancing community. For more information, please visit http://nextleveldancing.com

Jessika completed her Master's degree in teaching/instructional design and her undergraduate work in business management/leadership at Johnson & Wales University in Providence, Rhode Island. She has been named a "Forty Under 40" by the Columbus Business First organization and "Top Ten Business Coach" by the Boston's Women Business Journal.

As she launches the Next Level Dancing program, Jessika has dedicated herself to teaching workshops, speaking, writing and doing media interviews around these breakthrough strategies. She is busy completing her second book "Competing Like a Pro," which will be available in 2012. Jessika grew up in Gothenburg, Sweden and now resides in Columbus, Ohio with her beloved Scottish Terrier, Mac.